Also available from Continuum

Schools and Communities – John West-Burnham, Maggie Farrar and George Otero
Personalizing Learning – John West-Burnham and Max Coates
Transforming Education for Every Child: A Practical Handbook – John West-Burnham and Max Coates
System Leadership – Pat Collarbone and John West-Burnham
Rethinking Educational Leadership – John West-Burnham

Education for Social Justice

Achieving wellbeing for all

Laura Chapman and
John West-Burnham

continuum

Continuum International Publishing Group

The Tower Building	80 Maiden Lane,
11 York Road	Suite 704
London	New York,
SE1 7NX	NY 10038

www.continuumbooks.com

© Laura Chapman and John West-Burnham 2010

British Library Cataloguing-in-Publication Data
A catalogue record for this book is available from the British Library.

ISBN: 9781855394698 (paperback)

Library of Congress Cataloging-in-Publication Data
Chapman, Laura, 1968–
    Education for social justice: achieving wellbeing for all/Laura Chapman and John West-Burnham
        p. cm.
    Includes bibliographical references and index.
    ISBN 978-1-85539-469-8 (pbk.)
    1. Education–Great Britain. 2. Social justice–Study and teaching–Great Britain. 3. Great Britain–Social conditions–21st century. I. West-Burnham, John, 1946–   II. Title.

    LA632.C44.2009
    370.11′50941–dc22

2009028160

Typeset by BookEns Ltd, Royston, Herts.
Printed and bound in Great Britain by Bell & Bain, Glasgow

Contents

Introduction

Britain is widely regarded, with some justification, as one of the great liberal democracies with a deep commitment to the rule of law, and a long tradition of protecting and securing the rights of minorities – of all types. It is perhaps one of the great ironies of history that Britain was the one place in Europe where Karl Marx could find refuge and a degree of political toleration yet the majority of the indigenous population suffered from the most appalling social and economic discrimination (which provided him with much of his inspiration, of course). The potential of ideas has never really worried the British – the possibility of social and economic equity becoming a reality is far more disturbing. Britain as a society is broadly tolerant of social disadvantage – child poverty is not seen as utterly unacceptable in a wealthy democratic society; there is tolerance of systemic discrimination based on social class, and perceived relative status and casual discrimination based on disability is a relatively minor concern for the majority. At the time of writing only two of the top 100 Financial Times companies are headed by somebody who is not a white male.

Government policy since 1997 has recognized the issue of social and economic injustice as never before, although with severe constraints, most importantly the need not to challenge or question a range of fundamental assumptions about the way British society operates. For examples, the importance of a low tax economy, the significance and role of historical institutions and the need to perpetuate them – even if it means exacerbating social disadvantage.

The Labour government that came to power in 1997 inherited levels of poverty and inequality unprecedented in post-war history. More than one in four UK children lived in relative poverty, compared with one in eight when Labour had left office in 1979. Poverty among pensioners stood at 21%. Income inequality had sharpened widely: in 1979 the net incomes of the top tenth of the income distribution were about five times that of the bottom tenth; by the mid-1990's that ratio had roughly doubled. (Hills et al., 2009, p. 2)

The central focus of this book is social justice in education. Education is a key vehicle for challenging social injustice; however, it equally has the capacity to deepen and maximize social disadvantage:

> ... improved educational performance seems to have done very little to reduce social and economic inequality. Poor educational performance seems to be a reflection of deep-seated deprivation and social dislocation. Some well funded and well-run institutions have made an impact on the life chances of their pupils despite these social and economic factors, but not many. (Leadbeater and Mongon, 2006, p. 7)

In their study of social inequality in Britain, *Freedom's Orphans*, the Institute for Public Policy Research (IPPR) found that:

> ... in just over a decade, personal and social skills became 33 times more important in determining relative life chances. At the same time, young people from less affluent backgrounds became less likely than their more fortunate peers to develop these skills. For those born in 1958 the connection between family background, personal and social skills, and success later in life was barely discernible. But for a significant proportion of those born in 1970, social immobility – the passing on of disadvantage through families – was clearly due to the connection between family background and personal and social skills. (Margo and Dixon, 2006, p. vii)

Social mobility is one of the classic expressions of an open society. A dominant theme of this book is to explore the wide range of attitudes toward social injustice; in Britain these seem to range from absolute rejection of any form of social disadvantage as intolerable and totally unacceptable in a civilized society through passive acceptance ('The poor are always with us') to the positive rejection of the possibility or desirability of equality and equity. There remains a significantly influential voice in education which argues that equity and excellence are incompatible – a belief often accompanied by assertions about the orbit of the Sun around the Earth and the fact that the Earth is flat and about 4,000 years old.

The issue is disconcertingly simple, inequality, however expressed, is really bad news for a society; Wilkinson and Pickett (2009) demonstrate in multiple ways that it is in unequal societies that the greatest social problems are found. Their research shows a consistently high correlation between equal societies and what might be called the 'good life'. In very broad terms unequal or highly stratified societies are much more likely to have highly dysfunctional aspects to their social lives. The countries with the highest levels of equality have directly equivalent low levels of social morbidity. With disconcerting consistency, the countries with the highest levels of equality thrive in ways that countries with high inequality can only imagine or aspire to in the very long term – if at all.

There are, of course, trenchant opponents of any notion that wellbeing and happiness are anything to do with schools in particular and education in general. They would argue that wellbeing and happiness are elusive qualities which should not be brought into the public domain; that focusing on them creates false expectations and that they are distractions from the real purpose of schools – the delivery of a curriculum and the achievement of standards. Coming as they do from the safety and security of middle-class ghettoes, one can at least recognize the basis of their case – the defence of class based interests. Our purpose in writing this book is to explore the possible ways in which educational provision can seek to redress the balance of inequality and injustice in a society in which social injustice is culturally, historically and socially entrenched.

We are very grateful to Ingrid Bradbury and Julia Hayes for their invaluable work in preparing the manuscript of this book.

Laura Chapman
John West-Burnham
April 2009

1

Setting the scene

The aim of this chapter is to give an overview of the rationale for our argument for tackling social justice within education, by outlining the current situation within the UK from the perspectives of equality, equity and social justice. These terms will be discussed and defined in detail in subsequent chapters, but in broad terms equality refers to perceived relative status; equity describes parity in terms of outcomes, and social justice is the generic term covering the ethical framework concerned with equity and equality. Social justice exists in the extent to which there is equality and equity in a society or community. These principles have been the concern of philosophers and social reformers for generations. They help explain the struggle for democracy, the abolition of slavery and the movement to secure human rights. However, it could be argued, compellingly, that the history of humanity is actually the history of inequality:

> In the 13,000 years since the end of the last Ice Age, some parts of the world developed literate industrial societies with metal tools, others developed only nonliterate farming societies, and still others retained societies of hunter-gatherers with stone tools. Those historical inequalities have cast long shadows on the modern world, because the literate societies with metal tools have conquered or exterminated the other societies. (Diamond, 1998, p. 13)

Diamond provides a graphic illustration of the type of thinking that underpins much of this book. He describes a conversation with a politician in New Guinea, Yali, during which he asked Diamond 'Why is it that you white people developed so much cargo and brought it to New Guinea, but we black people had little cargo of our own?' (ibid., p. 14). New Guineans are intelligent, resourceful and highly creative people. Their situation, their lack of 'cargo' is at the heart of human history.

History is the story of relative power and cumulative advantage – those able to exploit those without – and doing so with depressing consistency and increasing brutality across recorded history. Not only do the 'haves' exploit the 'have-nots' across societies, they exploit them within societies. As soon as one culture dominates, destroys or subdues another culture then inequality is the inevitable manifestation. By the simplest criteria, inequality is endemic to the human condition. What is deeply disturbing is the way that, across history, the exploited, the dominated and the ruled come to accept their situation as the way of the world and even accept spurious legitimation of their role or status.

The pivotal events of history can often be seen as reducing or increasing inequality and injustice. The Norman invasion of England in 1066 is one of the most striking examples in modern history of one society subordinating, marginalizing and oppressing another through the systematic theft and brutalization of the defeated. There have, of course, been many examples since. Within 50 years of the Norman Conquest virtually all of the traditional Saxon names had disappeared from England – it's not a good idea to name children after the defeated culture – the names of the victorious Normans still seem to predominate in the birth announcements in the so-called quality press – the contemporary house magazines of the Norman conquerors. One of the legacies on the Norman victory was the creation of a society in which privilege and advantage came to be seen as part of the natural order of things. The Battle of Hastings:

> ... wiped out overnight a civilisation that, for its wealth, its political arrangements, its arts, its literature and its longevity was unique in Dark Ages Europe, and deserves celebration ... Anglo-Saxon England stood out as a beacon. (Harvey Wood, 2008, p. 2)

The beacon was replaced by a hierarchical and bureaucratic system which institutionalized inequality through the structures and norms of the feudal system – English society has been tolerant of privilege and systemic disadvantage ever since. Just how tolerant of discrimination British society is, is revealed in the extent of the evidence of disadvantage presented later in this chapter. It does seem bizarre that we still have systemic inequality in the fifth wealthiest nation on Earth, with a tradition of social reform going back almost 200 years; a claim, however problematic, to be a society based on Christian values and a broad consensus that the role of government is to intervene to alleviate disadvantage.

It is perhaps bizarre that the countries that consistently do worst on any international comparative surveys – the USA and the UK– are the wealthiest and fifth wealthiest economies in the world respectively. It is more surprising when the very different political philosophies of the two countries are concerned – for example the National Health Service in Britain compared with medical provision in the USA. An explanation might be found in the Gini coefficient which measures the spread of incomes, in effect an inequality index. If 1974 is taken as 100 then in 1979 the index stood at 101, by 1991 it had risen to 136. It fell to 132 in 1994, rose to 141 in 2000, and stood at 140 in 2006. In real terms, inequality in 2006 was 40 per cent higher than in 1974.

There are many expressions, ways of measuring and different definitions of inequality; however it remains a stubbornly subjective phenomenon. What follows in this chapter is an attempt to demonstrate the multiple modes of inequality there are and how they can be measured in many different ways. Each section presents data culled from a wide range of sources and presented without commentary as far as possible. Rather than start with a definition of injustice and inequality what follows describes the reality.

Wealth and poverty

Growing disparity is not in dispute. In a special report on Britain (1/2/07) *The Economist*, hardly a mouthpiece for progressives, noted how income was 'distributed more unequally than in almost any big rich country except America'. Bar Switzerland, the UK is far less equitable that other European countries. The top 10% of income earners get 27.3% of the cake; the bottom 10% get 2.6%. Twenty years ago the average chief executive of one of the top hundred companies on the FTSE index earned 17 times the average employee's pay. By 2008, the typical FTSE boss earned 75.5 times the average, according to the Institute of Directors. The UK is sliding backwards. (Toynbee and Walker, 2008, p. 5)

Social mobility

The UK's growth in wealth equality has been the fastest among the world's 30 richest and most developed countries. But in 2005, when the organisation compiled its latest data, the UK remained a more unequal society than three-quarters of OECD countries with the richest 10% earning nine times more than the poorest 10%.
... over the last 30 years there has been a very rapid increase in inequality.
The report also found that in the UK new generations struggle to escape the income levels of their parents more than in almost any other country in Europe
There is less social mobility in the UK than in Australia, Canada and Denmark. In this respect it is similar to the United States and Italy. (Booth, 2008, p. 6)

A truth the government has never acknowledged is that it is almost impossible to have high social mobility, in which children rise and fall according to their own talents and character, unless a society itself is reasonably equal and fair. If the ladder is long and steep, few can climb it. (Toynbee, 2008, p. 31)

An open society is one in which individuals are limited by their own talents rather than by their background. (*Times* Leader, 4 November, 2008, p. 2)

Gender

In 2007 Britain came 11th in the World Economic Forum's Global Gender Gap Index. In 2006 it was 9th. The biggest decline in performance was in the ranking for equal pay, where Britain dropped 20 places to Number 81. On education the UK has closed the gender gap completely but that is still not being translated into equal pay or a more proportionate number of women in senior business roles. (There is one woman who is CEO of an FTSE 100 company: Dame Marjorie Scardino Chief Executive of Pearson and now [March 2009] one black man: Tidjane Thiam Chief Executive of the Prudential)

Global Gender Gap Index (The higher the ranking the narrower the gap)

1. Norway
2. Finland
3. Sweden
4. Iceland
5. New Zealand
6. Philippines
7. Denmark
8. Ireland
9. Netherlands
10. Latvia
11. Germany
12. Sri lanka
13. United Kingdom
14. Switzerland
15. France (Batty, (2008, p. 13)

The number of women on various lists indicating social power and influence:

Sunday Times Rich List: 1%
Vanity Fair New Establishment100: 9%
The Stage Theatre 100: 22%
Daily Telegraph 100 living geniuses: 15%

Media Guardian Top 100: 21%
Sunday Telegraph Arts 100: 18%
Evening Standard 1001 Powerful Londoners: 27% (*Observer Review*, 7 December, 2008, p. 5)

Child poverty

Overall about 14% of pupils in England get free schools meals, but 25% are living below the poverty line. Data compiled for the *Guardian* have revealed the gap between the proportion of children in families without work – the best available measure of poverty – and the proportion getting free school meals. In Hull the ratio is 31% poor children with 17.8% getting free school meals, in Darlington the ratio is 21% and 13.9%, in Liverpool 35% and 21.7% respectively. In Tower Hamlets the ratio is 53% and 42.8%; however in Rutland with only 7% poor children only 3.3% are receiving free schools meals – proportionately as disturbing as the other figures. (Curtis, 2008, p. 12)

The Department for Work and Pensions said the number of Children living in relative poverty had risen by 100,000 to almost 2.9 million before housing costs are taken into account, and 3.9 million when they are included, a rise similar to the previous year.

This means that 2.9 million children, 22.7%, live in poverty. This is in the context that in 1996/97 7.7% of national income was earned by the poorest 20% – in 2006/07 this had fallen to 7.2%. In 1996/97 the wealthiest 20% earned 40.9%; this had risen to 42.6% in 2006/07. (The top 40% earned 64.4%)

In 2006/07 the national overall median income was £377 – poverty is defined as 60% of this figure – £226. This represents a fall of £3 on the previous year compared to a rise of £6 per week for the wealthiest 20% – taking their weekly income to £597. (Seager, 2008, p. 6)

Social class

The report by the Institute of Public Policy on raising young people in Britain, *Freedom's Orphans*, makes grim reading. There is a widening gulf between the way the more affluent majority socialise their children and what happens to those with fewer resources. The children who don't have the same experience of socialisation are being permanently left behind.

We already know, from the dual studies of children born in a single week in 1958 and 1970 that social mobility weakened over a short period. There was an 84% chance that a child born into the richest quarter of the population in 1958 would no longer have been in that position by their early 30s. But almost half the babies born into wealthier families in 1970 would remain in the wealthier group.

The IPPR has identified that, over a dozen years, personal and social skills, such as self-control, self-motivation and an ability to get on with others became 33 times more important in determining children's futures than they had been before. In, 1958, those with low incomes were only marginally less likely to develop good social skills than the well off. But the 1970 cohort showed a big gap in these skills between the classes. (Russell, 2008, p. 5)

The overwhelming factor in how well children do is not what type of school they attend – but social class. A report shows what has often been said but never proved: that the current league tables measure not the best but the most middle class schools; and that even the government's 'value added' tables fail to take account of the most crucial factor in educational outcomes – a pupil's address.

This unprecedented project has revealed that a child's social background is the crucial factor in academic performance and that a school's success is based not on its teachers, the way it is run, or what type of school it is, but, overwhelmingly, on the class background of its pupils. (Taylor, 2006)

Life expectancy

A Man living in the Glasgow suburb of Calton has a life expectancy of 54. A man living in the Glasgow suburb of Lenzie (15Km away) has a life expectancy of 82 years. (World Health Organization, 2008, p. 53)

Health

- Poverty affects children's birth weight. One third of births with low weight are associated with economic inequalities.
- Children face far greater health risks if they are in disadvantaged families. For example, they are ten times as likely to die suddenly in infancy, 2½ times as likely to suffer chronic illness as toddlers, twice as likely to have cerebral palsy and over three times as likely to suffer mental disorders.
- Adults who suffered poverty as children are 50% more likely to have limiting illnesses. Adults who had low birth weight are over four times as likely to have Type 2 diabetes (associated with obesity) and 25% more likely to die from heart disease.

- Mothers who grew up socially disadvantaged are one-third more likely to smoke during pregnancy. They are also much more likely to be among those with low qualifications, who are more likely to smoke and less likely to breastfeed. (Hirsch and Spencer, 2007, p. 2)

Mental health

Since women are far more likely than men to occupy servile, low-paid or unpaid jobs and to have social roles which subordinate them – whether down the pub, where they are interrupted more than men, speak less often and act as an audience if there are men present, or whether taking low-status roles such as that of housewife – it is not surprising that they are also more likely to be depressed. Whilst there is some debate as to whether the relationship is as strong for major depressions – manic and unipolar – as opposed to minor depressions, it is one of the best-established and least-disputed data of Social Psychiatry that being in a low class is a major predictor of depressive symptoms in technologically developed nations.

Depression is also lined with the aftermath of losses of status, many of which are themselves linked to low income. Recent divorcees suffer more than those from intact marriages as do the recently and long-term unemployed. Those with few friends and intimates are also more at risk.

Taken as a whole, the close link between depression and low status or loss thereof strongly suggests that humans of low status are also more likely to have low serotonin levels. (James, 1998, p. 39)

The report lays out evidence to show that poor mental health is both a cause and a consequence of social, economic and environmental inequalities. Mental health problems are more common in areas of deprivation and poor mental health is consistently associated with unemployment, less education and low income or material standard of living in addition to poor physical health.

Greater inequality heightens status competition and status insecurity across all income groups and among both adults and children. (Mental Health Foundation, 2009, p. 1)

Disability

In 2001, 24 per cent of disabled people of working age had no qualifications compared to 16 per cent of non-disabled people, which contributes to the difficulties people with disabilities face in finding employment; in 2002, they were five times more likely than non-disabled people to be out of work and claiming benefits. In spring 2003, disabled people had an employment rate of only 49 per cent, compared with an employment rate of 81 per cent of those who were not disabled.

    ... while official measures put 35.1 per cent of households with disabled people in poverty, when account is taken of additional costs of disability this figure becomes 60.8 per cent. (Dixon and Paxton, 2005, p. 32)

The overall proportion of non-disabled people who had a job was 76 per cent. Because disabled people tended to have some unfavourable demographic and economic characteristics (older, less-educated), the average employment probability of disabled people would have been 7 percentage points lower, at only 69 percent, even if they had not been disabled. The actual employment rate among disabled people, including consideration of their disability characteristics, was only 29 per cent. So the average employment disadvantage associated with impairment- the reduction in their job chances- was 40 percentage points. (Berthoud, 2006, p. 2)

Access to higher education

Children from the wealthiest income bracket are more than four-and-a-half times more likely to go to a high-ranking university- one that asks for at least three Bs at A-level – than the average child in the UK ... and they are nearly twice as likely to go to university at all.

    54 per cent of Bristol University Students come from the top quarter of the UK's most affluent homes. 3 per cent of Bristol University students come from the bottom quarter of the UK's least affluent homes.

    The wealthiest group make up just 1.9 per cent of the population but 8.4 per cent of the students at the three-Bs- and above universities. Groups where the average income is £42,500 account for 23.8 per cent of the population but produce 51.4 per cent of students at these universities. The poorest categories form 21.8 per cent of the population make up less than 6.3 per cent of students in these universities. (Shepherd, 2009, pp. 1–2)

Any form of inequality has the potential to compromise and diminish the quality of individual and collective life. There is probably a multiplier effect at work here: as the level of inequality grows and as more aspects of a person's life are informed by the experience of inequality so the possibility of the potential of that person's life's being seriously compromised is increased along every dimension:

Because more unequal places are marked by a more conflictual character of social relationships – so they suffer not only more homicide, but also more violent crime, less trust, less involvement in community life, and more racism – we should see them all as part of a single continuum affecting the nature of social relationships away from the most affectionate end toward the more conflictual end ... (Wilkinson, 2005, p. 55)

Inequality, the absence of social justice, has profoundly dysfunctional implications for a society or local community in that it can become self-sustaining and so self-compounding.

For a species which thrives on friendship and enjoys co-operation and trust, which has a strong sense of fairness, which is equipped with mirror neurons allowing us to learn our way of life through a process of identification, it is clear that social structures which create relationships based on inequality, inferiority and social exclusion must inflict a great deal of social pain. In this light we can perhaps begin not only to see why more unequal societies are so socially dysfunctional but, through that , perhaps also to feel more confident that a more humane society may be a great deal more practical than the highly unequal ones in which so many of us live now. (Wilkinson and Pickett, 2009, p. 213)

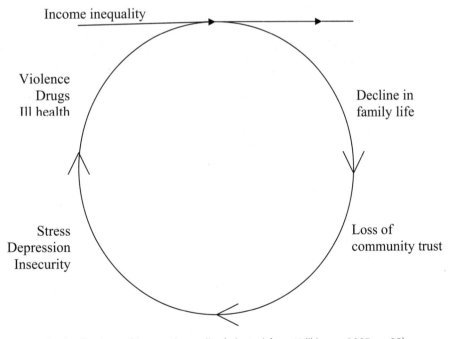

Figure 1.1 The implications of income inequality (adapted from Wilkinson, 2005, p. 23)

Just as a tornado's destructive power will increase exponentially when it merges with another tornado, so the cumulative effect of different types of inequality merging and becoming self-reinforcing is to initiate a downward spiral in which economic inequality exacerbates social inequality and so reinforces inequality, experienced as a personal phenomenon. It does appear to be the case that the implications of poverty and other manifestations of inequality are more severe and acute in Britain than in other advanced developed countries. The overall implication of these patterns of inequality is found in the stark differences between countries:

> The UK is ranked 13th, out of 22 European nations, when combining ratings for personal and social well-being, managing only 15th for social well-being and 13th for personal well-being alone.
>
> Although people in the UK are relatively satisfied with their lives, they score poorly on measures of vitality and sense of meaning and engagement.
>
> The UK comes 20 out of 22 nations on levels of trust and belonging ahead only of Slovakia and Bulgaria.
>
> For the 16–24 age group people in the UK report the lowest levels of trust and belonging. (www.nationalaccountsofwellbeing.org)

The existence of inequality is a denial of equity, parity and social justice, and this does seem to be a central issue in the lives of children in Britain:

> Britain and the US have more broken families than other countries, and our families are less cohesive in the way they live and eat together. British children are rougher with each other, and live more riskily in terms of alcohol, drugs and teenage pregnancy. And they are less inclined to stay in education.
>
> This comes against the background of much greater income inequality; many more children live in relative poverty in Britain and the US. (Layard and Dunn, 2009, p. 4)

Layard and Dunn draw radical and challenging conclusions from their analysis of the data:

> To produce better child outcomes we have to change the fundamental ethos and this will produce better child outcomes of all kinds. We must reduce inequality, but it is not enough. We must also change the overall ethos of our society, making it less success-orientated and more generous with respect. What we are talking about . . . is the law of love. (ibid., p. 135)

Education and social justice

Sadly, because social justice is perceived as such a vast challenge, for many in education it is still regarded as beyond their remit or possible influence. However, by not taking action to address the endemic unfairness of the education system, inequality remains and becomes accepted at a profound level by learners, teachers, leaders and administrators. With this in mind, there is no place for neutrality on the issue and with a deeper understanding of social justice there is the potential for an acknowledgement of personal and professional responsibility and so action. Early years settings, schools, colleges and universities have a huge part to play in shaping participants attitudes towards, and knowledge of, social justice.

Therefore, it is imperative for those working in education to understand that advocating social justice needs to be expressed more comprehensively through policy and practice rather than solely in curriculum content or shallow differentiation techniques. Organizing learning in ways that demonstrate equality requires clear thinking about changes in social and cultural ideology. Otherwise there is no imperative to act or define purpose in challenging the ways the system discriminates. So there is a need for educators to find ways of changing the learning environment so that policies and strategies articulate more clearly a philosophy of equality and inclusive practice.

> Another major force for reform around the Western world in the 1960s was the various forms of civil rights movements, pinpointing scores of inequities. Numerous national initiatives across the world focused on the disadvantaged. The education system was thought to be one of the major societal vehicles for reducing social inequality. To the intrinsic complexity of changing one's practice was added the enormous difficulty of tackling power structure and overcoming prejudice and ignorance of ethnic, class, gender and special difference of all kinds. (Fullan, 2007, p. 6)

So clearly, 'doing what we have done – better' is not the answer, perfecting a system that discriminates only increases inequality. This is why we believe that those involved in the education of young people need to understand more clearly the potential for their practice to discriminate, they need to be able to place their own work in context and understand the variables that mediate and inform the impact of their professional practice. On the one hand, the problem is perceived as situated in the part of the population that is underachieving. This enables blame and resentment to be directed towards that group. On the other, there is a realization that all participants within the system are under pressure and in need of attention, but the whole are somehow 'robbed' if the resources are going to disadvantaged sectors. The challenge is in having to decide who needs *most* help, support and resources, and in what way. In short, does education address the minority issue, or the whole system? This approach artificially polarizes the debate: in fact action is needed from both perspectives to secure the health of the whole.

The overarching problem

In a nutshell, most education systems directly affect the wellbeing of each participant by delivering in a way that is based on generic classifications – e.g. social class; artificial models of ability; restricted criteria of academic success which lead to uniform systems which take little account of personal uniqueness and identity. In a sense, the process and structures of schooling presupposes uniformity and a homogeneity that does not exist, in a system that imposes an arbitrary order, which in turn creates a hierarchy of value, status and significance. It is the underlying idea, that education teaches learners to know their place, that is rarely questioned. However, it is the perception by individuals of their place within the hierarchy that creates stress, and if it remains unchallenged will lead to wider social problems.

Creating more strategies designed to raise standards in the more academic subjects will not necessarily increase overall success for all learners. Concentrating on academic subjects deemed more important may limit the status and value of certain careers, and devalue others. Marginalizing career pathways and perpetuating the idea that some jobs are less worthwhile than others devalues and marginalizes the people within them. Phrases such as 'I'm only a childminder/carer/physio' epitomizes the perceived low value and self-worth of those within certain professions.

To show that society values every learner, it needs to find a way of widening opportunities for all learners, not just the academically motivated. People need to feel they can achieve in more flexible ways, so while providing for increasing specialization, education urgently needs to address parity of esteem. Unless education can treat all learners differently, it will fail to equip young people with the skills they need to do well in today's global society, and more fundamentally it will not enable them to value each other as equals.

> Although the source of blame varies, it is now an undeniable conclusion that the education system and its partners have failed to produce citizens who can contribute to and benefit from a world that offers enormous opportunity, and equally complex difficulty finding one's way in. (Fullan, 2007, p. 7)

In this culture of complexity, by imposing ageing structures that cannot adapt to changing pressures, education fuels a social dynamic of deepening inequality.

By classifying subjects into areas that are perceived as more or less useful, people that do well within different categories are perceived as more or less able.

> We have developed institutions and intellectual hierarchies on the assumption there are two types of people in the world, academic and non-academic: or as they are often called by common sense, able and the less able. (Robinson, 2001, p. 7)

The system has evolved to maintain hierarchies that in turn divide and marginalize people by streams, sets and bands. A culture of league tables, quantitative outcomes, targets and standards further compound the negative forces that marginalize the 'less able'. The way we categorize each other plays out on a social level: those we perceive as less capable, we identify as less important.

The design of the English education system reinforces a belief that high academic achievement leads to happier lives, and the legacy of a manufacturing economy still influences our perception of social success. Although a good education, i.e. academic success, is an indicator of life chances, this perspective is far too narrow, and there are other factors such as respectful, connected and meaningful relationships that cannot be determined in these terms. As we will see later, evidence shows that health and happiness are not improved if access to educational opportunity leads to a greater perception of inequality.

> As the technological revolution gathers pace, education and training are thought to be the answer to everything. They are, but we have to understand the question. Educating more people – and to a much higher standard – is vital. But we also have to educate them differently. The problem is that the present expansion is based on a fundamental misconception: the confusion of academic ability with intelligence. For years academic ability has been conflated with intelligence, and this idea has been institutionalised into testing systems, examinations, selection procedures, teacher education research. (Robinson, 2001, p. 7)

Institutions that focus primarily on raising standards by increasing grades, at the expense of enjoyment and holistic development, can only fail in achieving greater equality for all. If the aim of education is to enable learners to work towards a more equal society, then improving *schooling* can only make matters worse.

The world's economies and businesses, emerging from a period of increasingly rapid and significant change, need a new set of behaviours and skills. Young people leaving education will need to demonstrate adaptability in dynamic and complex environments. At a personal level, they need to acquire, develop and secure skills behaviours and strategies. This knowledge also needs to have significant personal meaning so that they can feel confident adapting ideas in different situations. At a social level, their attitude needs to translate into behaviour that demonstrates both tolerance and acceptance of different perspectives within a culture of increasing diversity.

Promoting uniqueness and growth in learning

As learners, people need to be understood as complex individuals with a multitude of perspectives and sensitivities. Growth and development are far from linear and, in practice, learners need to be taught in a way that says they are an equal but unique part of a wider whole.

> Human culture is as rich and diverse as it is because human intelligence is so complex and dynamic. We all have great natural capacities, but we all have them differently. There are not two types of people, academic or non-academic. We all have distinctive profiles of intellectual abilities with different strengths in visual intelligences, in sound, in movement, in mathematical thinking and the rest. Academic education looks only at certain sorts of ability. Those who have it often have other abilities that are ignored, those who don't are likely to be seen as not intelligent at all. (Robinson, 2001, pp. 9–10)

The human cost of a narrow definition of intelligence is huge, as it will have a long-term negative impact on young people's belief in their own capacity for growth and consequently damaging for their self-esteem. As research by Dweck (2006) shows, the impact of a belief in fixed ability stifles effort in all learners, even the high achievers. More worryingly it leads to an overall tendency towards disengagement in learners which fuels underachievement in every learner, and is actually toxic for certain groups.

The impact of systemic division, exemplified in sets and banding, will impact on the way we treat each other. Primarily, the consequence of physical separation according to ability affects relationships at all levels. If people are not valued or do not feel they belong to a wider whole, they are less likely to be treated as equals within the group or community. In the long term, the marginalization and isolation for those at the bottom of the pile are likely to lead to social problems far greater than the failure to participate fully in education. In the short term, difficult behaviour is a likely result, where people feel unaccepted and unappreciated and their feeling of belonging is eroded and they withdraw or 'kick off'. Inevitably, the very presence of a hierarchy has a lifelong impact on effort, growth and engagement for every individual at every level within any community.

The very notion that intelligence can be expressed on a distribution curve is debatable, yet many educationalist still would have us believe so, and they develop their practice to favour those at the top of this arbitrary hierarchy. Education has gained enormous insights into the dynamic and diverse nature of intelligence, with current research challenging conventional views of learning. However, our methods of teaching and testing still operate within a fixed, academically focused mindset. Education still appears to deliver a uniform, broadly academic curriculum to age-standardized ability, irrespective of personal growth, circumstance or background. Put simply, the learner is supposed to fit the system, not the other way around.

> The conflation of academic ability with intelligence is simply taken for granted. It is in this sense an ideology. Like many ideologies, this one persists despite all evidence of the contrary ... academic ability is essentially a capacity for certain sorts of verbal and mathematical reasoning. (Robinson, 2001, pp. 80–1)

If the purpose of education is to support the development of intelligence, and we understand that intelligence is multi-faceted, then this needs to be articulated within system change by developing practice that is both responsive and flexible enough to reflect this.

Understanding the implications of inequality

From our emerging perspective of establishing equal value for each learner, promoting a sense of unity for any group or community as a whole is pivotal. Therefore, policies, strategies and practices that divide or exclude need to be re-evaluated in terms of the extent to which they promote hierarchy or integration. For example, framing equality in relation to social inclusion or exclusion is missing the point since it implies forms of exclusion, according to social hierarchy, are somehow acceptable and therefore natural. Finding articulation in more holistic models, in term of inclusion and establishing belonging as fundamental, expresses much more deeply a sense of connection.

> Just as ecology is the study of the relationship between living beings and their environment, human ecology examines the relationship between human systems and their environment. Concerns about worker health, living wages, equity, education, and basic human rights are inseparable from concerns about water,

climate, soil and biodiversity. . . . it can be summed up in a single word: life. Life is *the* most fundamental human right . . . (Hawken, 2007, pp. 67–8)

The idea of prioritizing conditions that support holistic theory and practice are further developed by Michael Fullan in the context of successful educational change. He argues that the elements needed for achievement are multidimensional and well-balanced. We need to attend to more than one specific outcome, and this requires considering complexity and variation from the start. He talks about the whole learner in terms of addressing the three basics: literacy, numeracy and 'wellbeing':

> Wellbeing serves as a double duty. It directly supports literacy and numeracy; that is, emotional health is strongly associated with cognitive achievement. It also is indirectly but powerfully part of the educational and societal goal of dealing with the emotional and social consequences of failing and being of low status. In this sense political leaders must have an explicit agenda of wellbeing, of which education is one powerful component. (Fullan, 2007, p. 46)

Fullan is here questioning the marginalizing of wellbeing in the educational agenda. While there is no reason to suspect that wellbeing has been deliberately ignored or put in jeopardy through practice, if outcomes are seen as purely academic, this increases the risk of not valuing the practice that ensures learners feel better off. If equality and wellbeing are not central to practice, they will be seen as the marginal rather than a fundamental part of the learning process. This fragmentation of physical, social growth and intellectual development can only weaken connections and impoverish the learning experience.

> Once the unequal form of relations between young people at school becomes substantiated and objectified in educational qualifications, the trajectory of education, as a specific kind of structuring force, is established. For young people, the end result is a relatively higher or lower position in a social structure . . . (Evans, 2006, p. 10)

If all participants understand how they can benefit from a more holistic model of learning, they will feel less fearful and more confident of their role in change. That means taking responsibility for progress, broadening criteria for personal achievement and enabling people within the system to participate in the process. Above all, this will involve challenging our academic view of educational success in favour of something more holistic, multi-dimensional and long term, by addressing underlying ideology.

Education models the social hierarchy in quite specific ways, partly due to the fact that as a system it has aged without adapting to new demands in a period of rapid social change. Although schools are changing, in some ways change has been at a shallow, almost cosmetic level. Too few participants are enabled, given time or resources, to consider the question of moral purpose, therefore are unable to consider a deeper perspective.

> Big ideologies arose in the nineteenth century, and dominated our beliefs about what was true, false, and even possible into the twentieth century ... Because we are educated to believe that salvation is found in doctrines of a single system, we are naively susceptible to dissimulation and cant. Ideologies prey on these weaknesses and pervert them into blind loyalties, preventing diversity rather than nurturing natural evolution and the flourishing of ideas. Ecologists and biologists know that systems achieve stability and health through diversity, not uniformity. (Hawken, 2007, p. 16)

If we use a river as an analogy, a town will experience problems downstream because of debris, pollution and clutter at the river's source. Rather than build dams and weirs to control the pollution well down the river's course, is it not better to remove the pollution, literally, at source? Education can be seen as having built so many filters, dams and gates to control the flow that the river has become a totally artificial construct – it has lost its essential integrity. We are learning that to ignore the natural rhythms and balance of the river system is to invite disaster.

Recognizing the whole – specialization without division

Wholeness has become a predominant theme across a wide number of areas, from community work, spiritual growth, conservation issues and massage techniques; its relevance extends beyond education. There is little doubt that this is as a response to the fragmentation of traditional human relationships imposed by a highly specialized workforce in a highly mobile world. Wholeness and the spirit of connection have also become ways of conceptualizing belonging, and are critical ideas in defining the wider perspective on social justice:

> In Franklin Harold's book the Way of the Cell, he points out that for all its hard rationalism, molecular science asks us to accept a 'real humdinger ... that all organisms have descended ... from a single ancestral cell'. That primordial

connection, so incomprehensible to some yet so manifest and sacred and incontestable to others, links us inseparably to our common fate. (Hawken, 2007, p. 189)

We have marginalized the importance of our links to a greater whole, but in a period of world crisis the idea will become invaluable in the development of strategies for our very survival:

> There is no question that the environmental movement is critical to our survival. Our house is literally burning, and it is only logical that environmentalists expect the social justice movement to get on the environmental bus. But it is the other way around: the only way we are going to put out the fire is to get on the social justice bus, and heal our wounds, because in the end there is only one bus. Armed with that growing realization, we can address all that is harmful externally. (ibid., p. 190)

So not only are these ideas important for the wellbeing of young people within the education system at the present time, but insuring their understanding of the personal and shared implications of a sense of community, interdependence and equality of opportunity in the long term.

In an effort to conceptualize the idea of this integrated holistic approach we are using the shell as an analogy. At the central point of the shell is an individual point in isolation; as the spiral grows in complexity so it becomes more interdependent and so stronger. The beauty is that there is not a defining line between the parts of the ever-widening circle; every stage is connected to the next part of the shell and also connected to an ever-growing whole, either directly or through their connection to other parts of the shell.

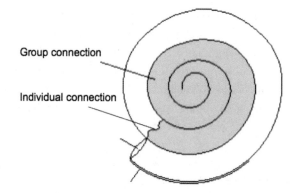

Figure 1.2 Strength through interdependence

The overall strength of the shell (department, school or community) depends on the strength of relationships. In Putnam's (2000) terms, behaviours that strengthen individual relationships are bonding whilst behaviours that strengthen group relationships are bridging. However, if the overarching aim is to increase the wellbeing of every part, the first step is to recognize they are all equally important to the whole, and that every relationship is significant to overall success. How we engage in bridging and bonding behaviours will be the key to diminishing the effects of inequality by flattening the artificial hierarchies created through the abuse of power over millennia and by challenging the social customs and mores that reinforce and lend credibility to systemic and institutional discrimination.

2 Social justice and education

The antithesis of social justice is inequality. In this particular usage the usual and specific focus of justice, equality before the law, is extended to all aspects of life in society. Thus the focus is on the concept of a just society in which there is parity in terms of social, political and economic matters as well as legal equality. The basic principle of the rule of law is applied to all aspects of being human. Hence the notion of equality before the law is extended to all dimensions of human interaction; nothing can supersede the fundamental criterion of common humanity. Not only does the idea of equality apply to all aspects of life but it is also rooted in the principle that:

> Each person possesses an inviolability founded on justice that even the welfare of society as a whole cannot override. For this reason justice denies that the loss of freedom for some is made right by a greater good shared by others. (Rawls, 1971, p. 3)

However, it is argued that it is not enough to be equal. There also has to be parity in terms of the measurable outcomes of living in society – back to Yali's question quoted at the beginning of Chapter 1 – it is not enough just to be equal:

> ... equity is not the same as equal opportunity. When practiced in the context of education, equity is focused on outcomes and results and is rooted in the recognition that because children have different needs and come from different circumstances, we cannot treat them all the same. (Noguera, 2008, p. xxvii)

In just the same way that it is now accepted as one of the key features of a modern democratic society that everybody is equal before the law; social position or influence should have no bearing on the legal process, so it is argued that all the other elements of social life should work to the same principle. Social justice has to be impartial; just as the statue of Justice on the Old Bailey in London is depicted as being blind, so social justice has to be rooted in fairness, nothing can compromise the essential parity that serves as the starting point for all social action. In essence it is not acceptable to have, for example, political equality if there is systemic poverty which diminishes and marginalizes people, and thereby inhibits or compromises social and economic equality. This raises the very challenging notion that in order to secure social justice it may be necessary to discriminate in favour of certain groups. This is Rawls' concept of the difference principle – the idea that inequalities are acceptable only to the extent that they benefit the worst off. Equality and equity have to be balanced. This point is powerfully exemplified by Mawson (2008, p. 144):

> Anyone who wants to know what equality means in practice has only to look around the poor-quality housing on our estates . . . Here everything is fair and equal – equally mediocre. Many of the politicians who represent the residents who live in this accommodation wisely choose not to live in the midst of such conditions.

Mawson goes on to make the explicit link between the principles of equality and the practice of equity:

> Social capital can only be created for the many when we move beyond a 'theological theory' of human life and grow a strong and honest sense of belonging and community, focused around a shared practical task. (ibid., p. 145)

Recognizing common rights to quality housing is not enough – there has to be a 'practical task' in order to achieve the equity that reflects the underlying equality; only then does social justice become a real possibility. The principle of equality has to be reinforced and extended by the practice of equity. On the basis of the discussion so far, three broad principles about the nature of social justice will inform the rest of this chapter and the book:

1 Equality: every human being has an absolute and equal right to common dignity and parity of esteem and entitlement to access the benefits of society on equal terms.
2 Equity: every human being has a right to benefit from the outcomes of society on the basis of fairness and according to need.
3 Social justice: justice requires deliberate and specific intervention to secure equality and equity.

The implications of the model set out in Figure 2.1 are very simple. Social justice only exists in the extent to which the principle of equality is reflected in the actual concrete experience of all people found in any given social situation, and that

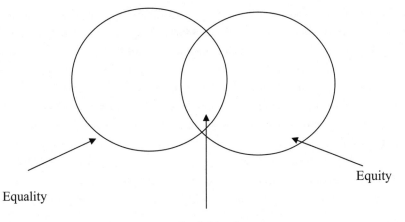

Equality

Social justice

Equity

Figure 2.1 Equality, equity and social justice

experience has to be measured in the extent of equity in outcomes. The more the two elements are integrated the greater the level of social justice, i.e. in the figure the more the two circles overlap the greater is the potential for social justice.

When we consider the nature of social justice, Rawls' principles lead us to two fundamental assertions. First, being inviolable, social justice cannot be diluted, diminished or denied – either there is social justice or there is not. Second, the principle applies to all dimensions of a person's life. An individual may or may not become involved in the legal system and if they do they will have the protection of the rule of law. However, social justice applies to every aspect of daily life, not just the special or extraordinary circumstances. Social justice moves us from the theoretical or ideal into the practical – the right to vote has to be paralleled by the right to associate, debate, etc., but it will only be meaningful in a society that is not controlled by economic or social minorities working to serve their own purposes.

There are numerous potential objections to this position. At a philosophical level there is a real intellectual debate about the extent to which it is possible to be confident in any claim to an objective standard of justice. The term is simply too contingent on time, place and power relationships. Equally there are those who would argue that any model of social justice will simply be a social construct used to justify/ attack the prevailing hegemony. The possibility of social justice will be dismissed by some as essentially utopian in nature. Most depressingly there are many advocates of an alternative perspective; covering a spectrum from free marketeers to the advocates of eugenics who argue that social justice 'interferes' with the laws of nature. It is perhaps worth pointing out that vaccination, immunization and creating a pure water supply all interfere with the laws of nature.

Advocates of the free market approach tend to point to countries that have a long-standing commitment to social justice and liberal democracy in order to demonstrate that they are often marginal to the world economy and lack access to the corridors of power. The fact that these countries (Japan, Sweden, Finland, Norway, Denmark and the Netherlands) have the highest levels of wellbeing, the most successful education systems, the lowest levels of mental illness and lowest prison populations seems to escape their critics. The neo-liberal preoccupation with performance, outcomes and efficiency does not, it would appear; necessarily lead to any of these characteristics. And yet the prevailing orthodoxy remains 'work harder' rather than ensure that equality and equity are in place because it is clear that they will have the greatest impact on performance. These concerns will be returned to throughout the following discussion.

However, one issue needs to be addressed explicitly at the outset of any discussion about social justice. This is the point that is the *a priori* for every discussion has to be the fundamental dignity and value of every human being in *their own right*. There cannot be 'degrees' of humanity; there can be no caveats or conditions which might be used to qualify the essential identity and integrity of each person. Human dignity has to be understood in terms of being human without any artificial constructs or idealized models. Human dignity is not compromised by states of consciousness, relative wealth or perceived social status. The famous anti-slavery plaque issued by Josiah Wedgwood shows a bound slave under the question: 'Am I not a man and a brother?' Pivotal to the ending of slavery was the recognition of the humanity of those who were being enslaved. Acts of violence and war tend to end with the belated recognition of shared humanity. The greatest outrages against humanity begin with the systematic denial of the humanity of the intended victim. From ethnic cleansing to domestic violence to child abuse, the failure to recognize common humanity both enables and exacerbates the violence.

There are no comparative criteria which can be scientifically, legitimately or morally used to classify human beings as the basis for discriminatory treatment. Thus, gender, ethnicity, disability, relative measures of intelligence, varying degrees of athleticism, different artistic abilities, linguistic usages, and social and cultural norms have to be regarded as descriptions of difference – not as the basis for discrimination whether personal or institutional. This is profoundly challenging, as human beings often develop a sense of identity in contradistinction to other human beings – hence discrimination, prejudice, ethnic violence, politics and, when all else fails, war. But even if these extremes are avoided, it remains very difficult to contemplate a society that is free of discriminatory behaviour.

In the same way as in colonial settings, where it was possible for the members of the colonial power to carry on conversations totally ignoring the presence in the same room of members of the indigenous population, so sophisticated and relatively advanced societies can ignore some members of their society – those who are marginalized in a variety of profound ways:

> ... there is the problem of doing justice to people with physical and mental impairments. These people are people, but they have not as yet been included, in existing societies, as citizens on a basis of equality with other citizens. The problem of extending education, health care, political rights and liberties, and equal citizenship more generally to such people seems to be a problem of justice, and an urgent one. (Nussbaum, 2006, p.2)

One of the most powerful arguments against those who advocate different levels of rights or access to services is the issue of gradation – at which point does the severity of a person's impairment merit the oppression that comes with the categorization of 'disabled'? At which point can the articulation of a person's feelings be classed as problematic? Physical and mental differences presently lead to labelling if they are perceived to be outside the typical margins or, worse, not accepted as normal. The way society understands disability as a personal misfortune, rather than a denial of equity imposed by social restriction and lack of acceptance, is a powerful metaphor for the issues of creating a just society; there can be no threshold.

> A good analysis requires recognizing the many varieties of impairment, need and dependency that 'normal' human beings experience, and thus the real continuity between 'normal' lives and those of people with lifelong mental disabilities. (ibid., p. 92)

In a very real sense we all have special needs; we all exist on a continuum of physical and mental, social and personal wellbeing. Ageing is the one common experience where most of us will experience some movement towards one end of the continuum rather than the other. Social justice is defined by the extent to which there is the possibility of both equality and equity in responding to an individual's personal circumstances.

The movement towards social justice is as much about cultural mores as it is about legal entitlement. One aspect of such movement is the concept of proportionate intervention or support. This is an aspect that many in the British tradition find unsettling. In essence the argument is that the greater the level of disadvantage the greater the level of intervention that is needed to secure entitlements and so justice.

In very practical terms a society committed to social justice would ensure that every child grows up experiencing the optimum levels of wellbeing. In many ways wellbeing is the dominant concept for the rest of this discussion, as it encapsulates what we understand as social justice for children and young people. A socially just society ensures that every child, irrespective of social background, parentage, post code or any variable, has an entitlement in terms of equality and equity to the benefits of growing up in a modern, democratic and affluent society; because if this is not the case then the alternative is to justify privilege, elitism and, frankly, the luck of birth. It might be possible one day to overcome the genetic lottery of conception; there are, of course, numerous moral issues associated with that possibility. However, we know that it is now possible to overcome the social and economic lottery of birth by creating a just society in which children grow and develop. The United Nations Convention on the Rights of the Child (CRC):

> ... gives children rights to, *inter alia*, freedom of expression, association, thought, conscience and religion, protection against abuse and violence, enjoyment of the highest attainable standard of health, education, rest and leisure, protection from economic exploitation and hazardous work.
> The CRC is important in the following respect. It represents children as the subject of rights. Children are recognised in a major international covenant as moral and legal subjects possessed of fundamental entitlements. (Archard, 2004, p. 54)

The UK formally ratified the Convention in 1991 but with significant reservations. The UK accepted the Convention in full in September 2008 – which might help to explain why social justice for children is not embedded in our national consciousness – as a society we have had reservations about children's rights.

Britain tends to see rights only in relationship with responsibilities – every benefit incurs an obligation. What is challenging for many is the idea that rights exist without reciprocal duties, essentially as inalienable, existing without condition or caveat. To avoid the deeper recesses of the rights–responsibilities debate, it is proposed to proceed on the basis of social justice as wellbeing. If social justice is embedded in a society then there is a high probability that a substantial proportion of young people will experience wellbeing. This is demonstrated in the UNICEF report discussed below which demonstrates a high correlation between levels of wellbeing and social policies committed to social and personal wellbeing. In reviewing the relative performance of education systems in Organization for Economic Co-operation and Development (OECD) member states there is a compelling link to be found between performance and social values:

> The high quality and performance of Finland's educational system cannot be divorced from the clarity, characteristics of, and broad consensus about the

country's broader social vision ... There is compelling clarity about and commitment to inclusive, equitable and innovative social values beyond as well as within the educational system. (Pont et al., 2008, p. 80)

It is hard to imagine how Finland's educational success could be achieved or maintained without reference to the nation's broader system of distinctive social values that more individualistic and inequitable societies may find it difficult to accept. (ibid., p. 92)

It would clearly be nonsensical to try and emulate the history and psyche of a country, we cannot become Finland. However it might be worth exploring those elements of Finnish society that are replicable or transferable. Of these a commitment to the wellbeing of all would seem to be a valid starting point. This is not to say that the use of wellbeing is unproblematic:

Wellbeing is a useful word because it is relatively unfamiliar. The *Oxford Dictionary of Quotations* has dozens of entries for happiness and happy. There is not a single one for wellbeing. It is not even clear how to spell it: wellbeing or well-being? Similarly in spoken English it is not straightforwardly obvious how to use the word. You can say, 'I am happy', but what would be the equivalent construction in relation to wellbeing? (Vernon, 2008, p. 44)

As a general principle wellbeing is a non-controversial concept, it is like thriving or flourishing when talking about a child's health – a good thing. As the basis for educational policy making and the moral foundation for educational leadership it is rather more challenging perhaps. Although the concept of wellbeing is well understood in everyday usage, it is important at this stage to provide an explicit definition that will inform subsequent discussion and review. Layard and Dunn (2009 p. 9) provide a powerful starting point for this discussion:

Flourishing means above all social engagement and the enjoyment of life – fulfilling our capacity to live in harmony with others and ourselves. Children flourish when they have a sense of meaning in their lives, which comes both from social engagement and from enthusiastic development of their own interests and talents. Children need both inner and outer harmony. These complement each other: outer harmony comes from a spirit of giving and inner self-worth makes getting less of an imperative.

Although the word wellbeing is not explicitly used here, the principles underpinning this view are consistent with the models that follow. Inevitably this discussion comes down to relative values and cultural differences, however within a Western orthodoxy certain manifestations of wellbeing do seem to be consistent. A powerful, contemporary and authoritative definition of wellbeing is provided by Alexander (2009 p. 30) in the proposals for the future of primary education developed by the Cambridge Primary Review:

> Wellbeing. To attend to children's capabilities, needs, hopes and anxieties here and now, and promote their mental, emotional and physical wellbeing and welfare. Happiness, a strong sense of self and a positive outlook on life are not only desirable in themselves; they are conducive to engagement and learning. But wellbeing goes much further than this, and 'happiness' on its own looks merely self-indulgent.

Alexander goes on to specify the components of wellbeing:

- attending to physical and emotional welfare
- wholeheartedly engaged in all kinds of worthwhile activities and relationships
- maximizing learning potential
- attending to future fulfilment as well as present needs and capabilities.

Central to the Cambridge Primary Review's proposals is the notion that:

> Wellbeing is thus both a precondition and an outcome of successful primary education. (ibid., p. 30)

These points are very powerful echoes of the principles that underpin *The Children's Plan* (DCSF, 2007b, pp. 5–6):

- government does not bring up children – parents do – so government needs to do more to back parents and families;
- all children have the potential to succeed and should go as far as their talents can take them;
- children and young people need to enjoy their childhood as well as grow up prepared for adult life;
- services need to be shaped by and responsive to children, young people and families, not designed around professional boundaries; and
- it is always better to prevent failure than tackle a crisis later.

These principles serve to reinforce and translate into specific strategies the broad aspirations of the *Every Child Matters* framework in England:

When we consulted children, young people and families, they wanted the government to set out a positive vision of the outcomes we want to achieve. The five outcomes which mattered most to children and young people were:

- **being healthy:** enjoying good physical and mental health and living a healthy lifestyle
- staying safe: being protected from harm and neglect
- enjoying and achieving: getting the most out of life and developing the skills for adulthood
- making a positive contribution: being involved with the community and society and not engaging in anti-social or offending behaviour
- economic well-being: not being prevented by economic disadvantage from achieving their full potential in life. (HM Treasury, 2003, pp. 6–7)

Much of the discussion in subsequent chapters is based around the five outcomes of Every Child Matters and the related principles of *The Children's Plan* (DCSF, 2007b). Together they come as close as any legislative framework ever has in England to articulating a child's entitlement to a quality of life which is based on equity and equality.

Another significant model of wellbeing was developed by UNICEF in the report of the Innocenti Research Centre (UNICEF, 2007):

When we attempt to measure children's well-being what we really seek to know is whether children are adequately clothed and housed and fed and protected, whether their circumstances are such that they are likely to become all that they are capable of becoming or whether they are disadvantaged in ways that make it difficult or impossible for them to participate fully in the life and opportunities around them. Above all we seek to know whether children feel loved, cherished, special and supported, within the family and the community, and whether the family and the community are being supported in this task by public policy and resources. (p. 39)

The UNICEF model identified six component elements of wellbeing:

1. Material wellbeing; measures of relative income and poverty, households without work and reported deprivation.
2. Health and safety; health at birth and in infancy, preventative health services, e.g. immunization and safety in terms of accidents and injuries.
3. Educational wellbeing; levels of academic achievement at age 15, numbers staying in education to age 19 and transition to employment.
4. Relationships; the nature of the family, the quality of family life and the quality of friendships.
5. Behaviours and risks; healthy lifestyles, risk behaviours, e.g. substance abuse, sexual activity and experience of violence.

6. Subjective wellbeing; self-perception in terms of health, engagement with school and positive self-regard.

The publication of this report in Britain led to a frenzy of political point scoring, counter-accusation, denial, xenophobia and resignation to living in a country which has real difficulties with childhood.

Table 2.1 Child wellbeing in rich countries*

Material wellbeing	18/21	(Sweden)
Health and safety	12/21	(Sweden)
Educational wellbeing	17/21	(Belgium)
Family and peer	21/21	(Italy)
Behaviours/risks	21/21	(Sweden)
Subjective wellbeing	20/20*	(Netherlands)
Overall	21/21	(Netherlands)

* No data available for USA.

Table 2.1 shows the relative position of the UK for each dimension of child wellbeing, with the highest scoring country shown in brackets.

The top seven countries in the survey were the Netherlands, Sweden, Denmark, Finland, Spain, Switzerland and Norway. The bottom six were France, Portugal, Austria, Hungary, the US and the UK. The best advice to children would seem to be: be born in the Netherlands or Scandinavia, grow up in liberal-democrat countries and avoid permanent members of the UN Security Council at all costs.

One of the key problems with any attempt to generate data about wellbeing, let alone international comparative data, is the highly subjective nature of the concept and the multiple cultural perspectives that have to be recognized. Just as humour may not travel across national boundaries, so the concept of happiness may be problematic from one society to another. However, when trends and patterns begin to emerge then confidence grows.

The New Economics Foundation (www.neweconomics.org) argues that wellbeing is made up from a number of key factors. People need:

- a sense of individual vitality
- to undertake activities that are meaningful, engaging and which make them feel competent and autonomous
- a stock of inner resources to help them cope when things go wrong and to be resilient to changes beyond their immediate control

- a sense of relatedness to other people ... supportive relationships and a sense of connection with others.

All of the elements cited above play a role in ensuring that people feel that their lives are going well, although their importance may vary as circumstances change:

> ... high levels of wellbeing mean that we are more able to respond to difficult circumstances, to innovate and constructively engage with other people and the world around us. As well as representing a highly effective way of bringing about good outcomes in many different areas of our lives, there is also a strong case for regarding wellbeing as an ultimate goal of human endeavour. (www.nationalaccountsofwellbeing.org p1)

The National Accounts of Wellbeing uses the following model of wellbeing as the basis of its research:

Personal wellbeing:
- emotional wellbeing
  - positive feelings
  - absence of negative feelings
- satisfying life
- vitality
- resilience and self-esteem
  - self-esteem
  - optimism
  - resilience
- positive functioning
  - autonomy
  - competence
  - engagement
  - meaning and purpose.

Social wellbeing:
- supportive relationships
- trust and belonging.

Wellbeing at work:
- job satisfaction
- satisfaction with work–life balance
- emotional experience of work
- work conditions.

On the basis of this model it has become possible to provide very detailed comparative data for wellbeing across European countries. When social and personal factors are given equal weighting then the following ranking emerges:

1. Denmark
2. Norway
3. Switzerland
4. Sweden
5. Ireland
6. Finland
7. Austria
8. Spain
9. Netherlands
10. Cyprus
11. Belgium
12. Germany
13. UK
14. Slovenia
15. Portugal
16. France

(Countries 17–22 are all in Eastern Europe.)

These figures are obviously not directly comparable with those of the UNICEF survey; the criteria are different and the sample group is totally different, i.e. adult. However there is a potentially significant comparability in terms of the political, economic and cultural similarities between the first seven countries in this survey and the results of the UNICEF survey. There does appear to be a high correlation between a permutation of a commitment to social justice; a view that the role of the government is to intervene in order to secure the wellbeing of its citizens; and a economic model based on high taxation, high expenditure and high levels of wellbeing in a society.

What is clear from the two significant empirical surveys that are available is how any review of wellbeing has to move beyond the quantitative into the qualitative – wellbeing is a subjective and emotional phenomenon which involves a continuum of responses from childhood immunization to levels of trust to perceived self-esteem. If social justice is to have any meaning at all then it has to deal with the full spectrum of issues identified in this discussion so far. There can be little doubt that the human being who feels that his/her life is positive in every one of the criteria for wellbeing outlined above is probably a happy person:

> Even where happiness is not considered an important value, if two equally just policies were to be devised, one of which promoted the subjective wellbeing of the population and the other of which detracted from it, it seems reasonable to assume that the former should be adopted. Happiness is in that case relevant to the construction of a good or desirable society and even if it is not, it is central to the evaluation of social justice. (Burchardt, 2005, p. 244)

And yet we have the evidence that, in spite of greater wealth, far better health and freedom from fear for many, we are still not happy. If happiness is a crucial manifestation of wellbeing then is it really the case that we have to argue that social justice means wellbeing, which in turn means happiness; so the role of society, and particularly government, is to secure happiness. The American Declaration of Independence refers to the 'inalienable right' to 'life, liberty and the pursuit of happiness'. The English *Children's Plan* (DCSF, 2007b) refers to the imperative that children should 'enjoy' their childhood; it wisely makes no commitment to happiness; in fairness, it makes no commitment to love either, yet who would contest that unconditional love is central to any child's sense of wellbeing, and that learning to love is a fundamental element of becoming a whole person?

Vernon (2008, p, 131) takes the potential limitations of wellbeing and happiness to an altogether different plane:

> The good is simple, it is just very difficult. What can be secured, though, is a taste for the mystery of things, of transcendence that is unputdownable as it is indescribable as it is illuminating. We love beauty; we are drawn to the good. It is a vision of life beyond happiness and pleasure, rules and duty, even meaning and virtue – although they are all part of it. By seeking the good in life you find wellbeing.

Perhaps we need to learn to distinguish between those aspects of life which are common, shared, mutually understood and where there is a consensus that their presence is, normally, desirable to aspects of life that are highly personal, individual and subjective. In other words, we cannot legislate for every aspect of a person's life and potential happiness; but when we can do something that will enhance their happiness then we have a duty to do so.

It is neither desirable nor possible to produce one integrated model that synthesize all of the elements of the discussion so far. At the same time it is important to have some clear mapping of the territory to be covered in the rest of the book. Figure 2.2 shows how we perceive the relationship between all of the elements explored so far; this model serves as the basis for the structure of the subsequent discussion.

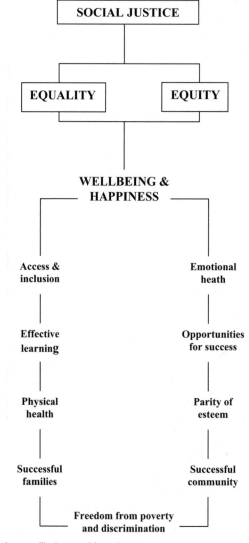

Figure 2.2 Social justice, wellbeing and happiness

3 Vulnerable children and marginalized groups

A clear understanding of the impact of social inequality on the health and happiness of vulnerable children is central to any debate about social justice. Evidence shows that environmental circumstances can have serious implications for life chances. The discrimination and poverty that many young people face can, particularly in the early years, be addressed in ways that will significantly improve outcomes for development and wellbeing.

Childhood experience and environment have a pervasive impact on life chances. While schools are limited to the extent they can influence their community context, they need to do a great deal more to help young people understand the forces that perpetuate social inequality.

By developing strategies that promote fairness, schools can have significant effect on their own environment and cultures. In the long term this will ensure a better start for children, as the negative pressures can be alleviated through supportive and understanding relationships, particularly early on. However, this demands insight and understanding of a specific nature by all of those who work with children. The problems of poverty and discrimination also tend to compound and reinforce each other. Understanding social inequality gives schools a clear route towards the reduction of the negative factors that affect vulnerable children. It indicates how they can intervene to expose unfairness and develop strategies that will both strengthen relationships and improve the social and economic environment.

> Depending on the nature of these environments, different groups will have different experiences of material conditions, psychosocial support, and behavioural options, which make them more or less vulnerable to poor health. Social stratification likewise determines differential access to and utilization of health care, with consequences for the inequitable promotion of health and wellbeing, disease prevention, and illness recovery and survival. (World Health Organization, 2008, p. 7)

The stratification outlined above – the social hierarchy –will indicate which groups are likely to face less favourable conditions. It is essential to understand the scale of the inequality; without this understanding, schools will be unable to identify those factors which they can intervene and thus influence and enhance children's wellbeing. Where wealth and deprivation exist cheek by jowl, an awareness of the level of local disparity is imperative in order to inform planning and appropriately focused strategies. In these communities there is an additional duty to concentrate effort on the most vulnerable children and for this to happen schools need to understand more clearly how to identify those particular individuals.

Poverty, inequality and status

Poverty in this country affects some groups of people much more than others. Here we concentrate on the fact that women and children are significantly more likely to be poor than men. Thirty percent of women have an income of less than £100 a week, compared to fourteen percent of men, and it is having a child that puts women at a particular risk of becoming poor. Four out of ten poor children live in households headed by a single mother and another three out of ten in households where the father is in employment but the mother has low or no income. (TUC, June 2008, p. 1)

The relationship between poverty and social status is often poorly articulated. As Toynbee and Walker (2008) explain, social class and poverty are linked but should not be equated. The first thing to understand is that, for many people, personal background often leads to unfair access to community resources such as housing, transport, education, leisure facilities and job opportunities. For many households, the negative impact of unpleasant surroundings, unfair wages and proportionally higher taxes creates an unbreakable cycle of poverty. Unfairness in wealth distribution creates an increasing discrepancy between different communities' environments that impact on the wellbeing of a growing proportion of households. According to the Department for Work and Pensions (DWP) 2006:

In the mid to late 1990s the United Kingdom suffered higher child poverty than nearly all other industrialised nations. Over a period of 20 years, the proportion of children in relative low-income households had more than doubled, one in five families had no one in work and one in every three children was living in poverty. In 1999 the Prime Minister pledged to eradicate child poverty in the UK within a generation.

Being in employment does not necessarily prevent child poverty. DWP figures show that 43 per cent of children in households where at least one adult worked live in poverty (Children in Scotland, 2006).

The factors underlying class inequality are far more complex. For many, restricted access to work is a significant factor and this is not helped by an education system that reinforces an outmoded 'worker hierarchy'. The system itself teaches a performance differential with accepted differences in pay which relate more to status than to effort or hard work (Toynbee and Walker, 2008). For many, pay is the significant factor that tips the balance into poverty. Insufficient pay for basic needs is a very real problem (particularly in the care and hospitality sectors) and can mean that, for many households, full employment can still mean poverty even where two adults are work.

In an important recent paper on low pay, the Institute for Public Policy Research noted that, in 2006, 16.1 percent of men in work were low paid, compared with 29 percent of women workers. 45.7 percent of part-time workers were low paid, compared with 14.2 percent of full-time workers. There are 1.4 million children in working households living in poverty – half of all poor children.

Low pay is an important cause of women's poverty, which is important because of its effects on women themselves and because of the effects on their children. The Government has a high profile commitment to ending child poverty in a generation, and the poverty of children is inextricable from the poverty of their mothers. (TUC, 2008, p. 2)

The impact of unfair wages, lack of family friendly work conditions and added pressures of sole childcare responsibilities further intensify the problem for single-parent households.

A low-paid job is often an untenable option for many lone parents and condemns many to the benefit trap:

Lone parents under the age of 25 account for just one in eight of all young adults in poverty and just a fifth of all the lone parents in poverty. The stereotypical image of a lone parent in poverty as a young, even teenaged, mum, is therefore quite wrong. Rather, most of lone parents in poverty are aged 25 or over and there are, in fact, as many over 40 as there are under 25. (Palmer et al., 2007, p. 12)

It is the blame culture fuelled by media bias that deepens the class divide – pay is another example of a polarized society. The ratio of pay between the richest fifth and the poorest fifth is a clear indicator of systemic unfairness. In Japan the ratio is 3.4:1; in Finland 3.7:1; in the UK it is 7.2:1; and in the USA 8.5:1. These ratios are reflected in the full range of social dysfunctionality. All of this perpetuates a vicious circle suggesting that ability and class can be equated, and that certain groups can be expected to achieve less.

Stereotypes and prejudice

Stereotypes are a filing system: they are a means of categorizing groups – the boxes in which we store and label information. To a large extent stereotypes help to make sense of the world, process information and keep track of the vast volume of difference encountered. Of themselves, stereotypes are neither good nor bad: the problem is that people then label their 'boxes'. 'Attractive, tall, people are able'; 'scruffy means disorganized'; 'poor children are more likely to fail' – and so on. It is not the label itself that damages, but the assumption that a label can determine ability.

These assumptions lead to prejudice (particularly in the predicted performance of certain groups) and reaffirm stereotypical beliefs. In this way, what may be viewed as 'common sense' in fact constitutes deeply held ideas that remain unquestioned. While prejudice justifies unfair behaviour in practice, it also perpetuates the problem – a deep-set belief reinforced by a label. Rarely are the conditions that create the prejudice explored or understood, and so diverse children receive different treatment. Those already vulnerable will be most affected, as they will arrive in school with their stereotypical label: 'poor', 'SEN', 'difficult', or even 'gifted'.

A poor understanding of inequality and poverty coupled with the prejudice associated with class stereotype damages the safety, wellbeing and potential of vulnerable children. Fuelled by negative images (for example, of the unemployed as lazy and work shy) the issue of parity is often ignored and blame is directed on those who must currently try hardest to achieve:

> It is the stereotypes associated with people from different backgrounds that need contradiction. The issue of potential will never be dealt with adequately if class status is not addressed more adequately in practice. (Palmer et al., 2007, p. 12)

Even before difficult circumstances are taken into account, a belief in stereotypes ensures the responsibility for underachievement is laid at the feet of the most vulnerable in our communities. Articulating equal value more clearly in action, and creating practice that increases fairness and celebrates effort, will ultimately break the cycle and change children's lives.

Stereotypes other than class can also influence opportunity and due to the system they impact on outcomes for marginalized groups at an increasing rate:

> At 30 per cent, the poverty rate among those aged 25 to retirement who are disabled is twice the rate for those who are not disabled. Though steady in recent years, this 'excess' risk for disabled people compared with non-disabled people is larger than it was a decade ago. (Palmer et al., 2007, p.12)

In the case of vulnerable children, the character of prejudice might vary, but there is an underlying assumption that they are perceived as less intelligent, capable, or able to achieve 'typical' expectations. This is reinforced by prevalent beliefs that intelligence is inherited and fixed, and that certain individuals from specifically identifiable groups are incapable of performance beyond certain targets.

> No one knows about negative ability labels like members of stereotyped groups. For example, African Americans know about being stereotyped as lower in intelligence. And women know about being stereotyped as bad at math and science. (Dweck, 2006, p. 74)

These stereotypical views are reinforced and compounded by school organization, systems and structures; subject timetabling, department administration and ability grouping play a part in potentially compromising performance, and if they are not significantly modified could lead to the underachievement and disengagement of young people. Even without addressing teacher prejudice, class organization lowers effort in the classroom which could lead to the internalized oppression of vulnerable children. There is evidence:

> ... that even checking a box to indicate your race or sex can trigger the stereotype in your mind and lower your test score ... just put more males in the room with a female before a math test, and down goes the score. (ibid., p. 75)

If this is the case, what will be the effect on children put through additional testing on the grounds of physical impairments or different cognitive ability?

The potential inconsistency in teacher understanding of what constitutes prejudice is disturbing because it translates into an inability to engage in reflective practice and so change that practice. If prejudice remains unchallenged then young people will learn that it is acceptable. For example, if racist language in the playground is punished, then sexist or disablist language should be equally challenged. All too often, teachers themselves are confused as to what constitutes abuse on the grounds of perceived relative ability. It is not uncommon for children to be removed from class for disruptive behaviour (even as a result of unfair treatment) while the causal prejudice often remains unaddressed, creating clear inequality in treatment. Obviously different teachers will react differently to stereotypes, and prejudiced attitudes and behaviour are as likely to manifest in good or bad people, educated or poorly educated, rich or poor, disabled or non-disabled.

4 Systemic discrimination and the rights of the child

It is vital that all those working with children and young people understand that every child has the right to a 'remedy of circumstance', i.e. for the alleviation of negative circumstances. It is not morally or professionally acceptable to argue for tacit complicity or mute acceptance. Educational establishments need to be more explicit in strategies for young people that class *does not* necessarily determine life chances but lack of opportunity *does*. Otherwise, the often unspoken belief that high academic achievers are somehow deserving of most praise, increased opportunity and greater rewards, will continue to justify systemic inequality. Vulnerable children are needy because their rights have been neglected, not because they have additional or different demands compared with other children.

One of the issues to emerge from Chapter 2 is the importance of the belief that all children have an equal capacity for effort, aspiration and potential. Sadly, however, as we have identified, these qualities can be eroded by prejudicial practice, negative attitudes and rigid systems. From a rights perspective, our concern is that unconscious assumptions, based on widely accepted stereotypes, can justify unfair treatment and lead to the denial of certain needs. Focusing on raising performance and reaching higher targets can neglect to make accommodation for personal difference and fail to address issues that reinforce inequality. This happens particularly when the action needed to provide for some children's needs feels counterintuitive to established teaching practice and methodology or school organization and policy.

In Britain, where deference to hierarchy and authority are so deeply ingrained, it is particularly difficult to challenge the *status quo*, let alone turn it on its head. If children from all backgrounds had the same opportunity and freedom from discrimination then the wellbeing of vulnerable children would not be in jeopardy. The legal and constitutional principles seem to be very clear and widely understood – unfortunately they are not translated into consistent practice:

Article 2
The child shall enjoy all the rights set forth in this Declaration. Every child, without any exception whatsoever, shall be entitled to these rights, without distinction or discrimination on account of race, colour, sex, language, religion, political or other opinion, national or social origin, property, birth or other status, whether of himself or of his family. (OHCHR, 2009)

The layering and variety of stereotypes can become a self-sustaining and self-reinforcing multiplier effect often adding to the justification for inequality in the public consciousness. Many marginalized individuals say they face a 'double whammy' or a commutative oppression, linked to the number of negative stereotypes with which they are identified. Not identifying or removing the cumulative barriers caused by this prejudice can be seen as a neglect of duty, as it imposes increased effort by certain children in order to achieve.

Inequity in the conditions of daily living is shaped by deeper social structures and processes. The inequity is systematic, produced by social norms, policies, and practices that tolerate or actually promote unfair distribution of and access to power, wealth, and other necessary social resources. (World Health Organization, 2008, p. 18)

The factors favouring positive outcomes, supportive relationships, shared values and rewarded achievement can be deliberately enhanced or introduced through policies and local strategies activity. Systemic discrimination not only puts vulnerable children at a disadvantage during childhood, but are then accepted, learned and rationalized as acceptable and typical in adult life:

Although 93 per cent of severely poor children live in households where adults cannot afford a holiday away from home for at least one week a year, 'only' 87 per cent of severely poor children do not get such a holiday.
51 per cent of adults in the households of severely poor children cannot afford to have friends or family round for a drink or meal at least once a month, but 'only' 29 per cent of severely poor children cannot have their friends round for tea or snacks at least once a fortnight.
45 per cent of children in severe poverty live in households where adults cannot afford a hobby or leisure activity, but 'only' 24 per cent go without a hobby or leisure activity themselves. (Magadi and Middleton, 2007, pp. 11–12)

The figures above make grim reading, as they clearly describe the absence of the factors that promote health and happiness. Without practice that focuses on embedding rights to play, rest, friendship and privacy, children have little chance of developing the skills and relationship that support wellbeing in the long term. Early years' settings, schools, colleges and universities may not have the capacity to affect the wider social problems affecting children. However, they can begin to redress issues of fairness within their own environment; not to do so would constitute neglect.

Because the pressures identified are systemic and ingrained at a deeper ideological level than merely the knowledge and intention of teachers, the resolution of inequality will require schools to go beyond superficial goodwill and developing a range of materials to support understanding. Redressing the balance will mean reassigning values, reassessing current practice and the reorganization of the learning organization.

Freedom from discrimination: questioning ability and status

There is an idea that it is some ways acceptable to marginalize and exclude vulnerable children. The key underlying problem here concerns how we work with hierarchical values. In schools, the relative position of children is established by academically orientated testing: a system that categorizes both teachers and learners along an academic continuum and which actively discriminates against the less able on any measure of ability. On the grounds of ability or status, schools may allocate resources unfairly, justify dismissive treatment and, in the worst cases, actually exclude. It is very important to measure and record just which pupils are systematically suspended and excluded and to identify any trends that may indicate systemic discrimination.

The system has evolved to maintain a belief in a continuum that divides learners and teachers into sets and bands. A culture of league tables, quantitative outcomes, targets and standards further compounds the negative forces that marginalize the 'less able':

> We have developed institutions and intellectual hierarchies on the assumption there are two types of people in the world, academic and non-academic: or as they are often called by common sense, able and the less able. (Robinson, 2001, p. 7)

Alarmingly, children as young as six draw links between ability, social status and physical traits such as attractiveness. They equate good looks to likeability and success – who is cool, trendy, mad, bad or sad. It is not hard to understand how celebrity status overrides the understanding of what is needed for happiness or long-term wellbeing. Children can be forgiven for being confused when they are surrounded by media images of the rich and beautiful, and success is rarely depicted in terms of relationships, values or engaging work. Evidence shows how deeply media affects young people's status and their acceptance of prejudicial norms:

> Levels of dissatisfaction amongst girls with their bodies are high and rising. Four in ten teenage girls surveyed by the magazine *Bliss* in 2005 said that they had considered plastic surgery. Two thirds of the 2,000 fourteen and fifteen-year-olds who took part in the questionnaire said that pressure to look 'perfect' came from comparing themselves unfavourably with celebrities. (Brooks, 2006, pp. 203–4)

Such dissatisfaction clearly emphasizes the significance accorded to attractiveness as a factor in lifelong success. From feeling less attractive to internalizing the feeling of being less able, children understand the effect stereotypes will have on their own future:

> She [Laura] just gets so frustrated with the way she looks. 'I think it's unfair that some people are born into life looking so much better that other people and they get treated better throughout their lives because of it.' She's sparring. 'And I feel like people are always going to judge me because I don't look as good'. (Brooks, 2006, pp. 203–4)

School organization and teaching methodology should be understood as prejudicial if it falls short of delivering to the needs of vulnerable children. Only deliberate reassessment of practice will prevent justification for the marginalization of learners according to ability. Particularly with respect to different theoretical, therapeutic models and ways of working, prejudicial practice is often subconscious and reinforced by different ideology. This makes discrimination particularly difficult to challenge, as it is easier to defend action based on typical practice, rather than confront deep-set ideas. However, without change the cost of discrimination will be in the quality relationships for those involved, and they have been identified as fundamental to present happiness and long-term wellbeing.

The education system's current preoccupation with performance has become an oppressive force that can easily lead to abuses of power within the learning relationship.. Where resources are justified by raising performance, a systemic marginalization of vulnerable groups decreases the likelihood of adults in teaching roles questioning their perspective or actions:

> The pressure on schools and on teachers to focus on measurements and comparisons of performance can obscure the emotional and interpersonal

experience at the heart of learning. Teachers can become preoccupied by performance and content, which can inhibit their capacity to focus on the emotional experience of learning. This can have a negative effect on school experience for pupils who may have experienced an adverse early relationship in which their needs may have been overlooked because of parental preoccupations or external pressures. (Geddes, 2006, p. 60)

While it is rarely articulated clearly, the oppression vulnerable children face is still expressed by the acceptance that certain groups deserve their place in the pecking order. If this were not the case, early years and special educational needs would enjoy a higher profile and fairer resources. As it is, the justification of special educational needs support in relation to overall achievement is still contentious. The nub of the issue remains around the perception that the allocation of resources to children with specific needs somehow steals resources from the rest. The silent acceptance of a linear continuum of academic ability allows unfair treatment in favour of the more able. It justifies leaving some young people to struggle without having all their needs met. Indeed, policy makers struggle with articulating fairness in guidance:

LAs [local authorities] have a general duty to educate a child in ordinary schools, as long as this is consistent with the parents' wishes and the child receives the appropriate special educational provision, and the child's inclusion would be compatible with the efficient education of other children. (Ofsted, 2006)

The oppression is so deeply rooted that it goes largely undetected and unchallenged in public consciousness. Vulnerable children, perceived as belonging to specific groups, often find it difficult to identify precise statements that characterize the prejudice. These children frequently deny discrimination, yet relate stories showing that they have clearly experienced it (Lumby, 2007). In essence, our system teaches young people to accept discrimination and, over time, what is expressed in language and practice is reinforced through the system. Alarmingly, these ideas are repeated throughout communities and workplaces in those same groups that fail to get jobs, whose work gets treated as second rate and are paid less as a result, and whose picture never appears in the company magazine. This unfairness, witnessed and experienced by children on a daily basis, is played out in playgrounds across the land. Before schools can say they are dealing with the issues of bullying, they need to address the underlying causes of inequality that lead to replication in the thinking and actions of young people:

Bullying is among the top concerns that parents have about their children's safety and well-being at and on the way to and from school. Bullying is also a top concern of children and young people themselves. Bullying makes the lives of its victims a misery: it undermines their confidence and self esteem; and destroys their sense of security. Bullying impacts on its victims' attendance and attainment at school, marginalises those groups who may be particular targets for bullies and can have a life-long negative impact on some young people's lives. At worst, bullying has been a factor in pupil suicide. (DCSF, 2007c, p. 8)

In an unfair culture, where academic performance determines hierarchy, prejudice is not only hurtful to some, but lack of development in practice will affect all children negatively:

There is also evidence that a substantial amount of bullying is fuelled by prejudice – racial, religious, and homophobic – and against children with special educational needs or disabilities or who are perceived as different in some way. We all have a shared responsibility to support schools in preventing and tackling bullying of all kinds and whatever its driver in order to protect the well-being of some of the most vulnerable young people and to promote stronger communities in which diversity is valued and the weak protected. (DCSFc, 2007, p. 4)

Interestingly, the area relating to disability and special educational needs was the last to be added to the government guidance on bullying.

The pressure of a performance-driven system, academic oppression, and the way adults hold power over young people, adds up to a form of bullying quite specific to education:

Children and young people have told the Commissioner that they deeply resent the negative way adult society views them: 'Teenagers are always seen as being thugs and bullies and you can't go into a shop without getting a funny look.' (Office of the Children's Commissioner, 2006, p. 7)

This bullying is often poorly articulated, rarely confronted and develops insidiously. It influences both wellbeing and subsequent life chances. Children learn that injustice on the grounds of ability is acceptable and sanctioned by adults themselves:

The question is whether there is something in the contemporary experience of childhood that makes bullying behaviour more likely. There is the fear that violence on screen makes children more aggressive towards one another. But if childhood is an experience of disempowerment, perhaps it shouldn't come as a surprise that some children misuse the only power they hold: over each other. (Brooks, 2006, p. 200)

The overall pressure of results and the separation of groups according to anticipated achievement exacerbate what is already a social problem for many. In this way the status often imposed by school organization makes vulnerable children more likely to become victims of bullying.

> Research shows that children and young people with SEN (special educational needs) and disabilities are more at risk of bullying than their peers .... Bullying related to appearance or health conditions. Those with health or visible medical conditions, such as eczema, may be more likely than their peers to become targets for bullying behaviour. (DCSF, 2007a, p. 41)

While the challenges faced by children outside school are sufficient to impact on health and happiness, the problems linked to low self-esteem caused by bullying can cause more serious disorders that damage social skills and interfere with learning:

> Interestingly, they turned this pressure on each other. Of the one in six who said they had been bullied, the majority had been harassed because of what they looked like. Only 8 per cent were happy with their bodies, while a quarter had suffered from an eating disorder. (Brooks, 2006, pp. 203–4)

A circle of hardship can easily emerge: learning problems arising from family circumstance and bullying are deepened through difficulty with engaging in learning activity. Educational organizations that fail to integrate emotional and cognitive needs in practice and strategic thinking that effectively values role and status above the person may well promote a culture of discrimination and bullying.

However, nothing is possible without deliberate strategies to promote relationships. Some schools have introduced separate outdoor spaces for individual year groups. Restricting the opportunity for older children to bully during break-time facilitates the development of closer relationships and enhances a sense of belonging within a specific group but it can inhibit the development of a whole school culture:

> Of course, bullying behaviour is not the preserve of childhood. Even with the buffer of maturity, a variety of Acts of Parliament, and recourse to tribunals, bullying does not stop at the school gates. The quest for status, the exploitation of difference and the pack mentality never absent themselves from our social interaction. But it is in the playground, where the relationship between instinct and self-control is still being tested, that the human capacity for cruelty as well as kindness is laid bare along with the old lie: stick and stones may break my bones but names will never hurt me. (Brooks, 2006, p. 200)

The negative implications for young people's relationships and the behaviour they adopt towards one another will continue into adulthood if it is not dealt with appropriately and consistently in the context of childhood. If inequality is not tackled effectively it will be felt most by those groups already stigmatized by society, and the implications of ignoring stereotypes will be devastating for certain children. The impact of teachers' expertise in dealing with prejudice and bullying can influence the definition of acceptable behaviour towards vulnerable groups – with lifelong consequences, as Wilkinson explains:

> The lack of social cohesion in the more unequal societies has multifaceted negative consequences, notably the tendency in 'societies with bigger inequalities to show more discrimination against vulnerable groups, whether women, religious or ethnic minorities' which 'is part of a wider process of downward discrimination in which people who feel humiliated try to repair their sense of selfhood by demonstrating their superiority over more vulnerable groups'. (2005, p. 21)

Developing a positive culture that places relationships at the centre of teaching activity can help reduce inequality. A sense of acceptance and belonging strongly influences the way in which children deal with discrimination. As exemplified by the SEAL (Social Emotional Aspects of Learning) programme, education can do much in this area by acknowledging the emotional and personal impact of inequality.

> Social, emotional and behavioral skills underlie almost every aspect of school, home and community life, including effective learning and getting on with other people. They are fundamental to school improvement. (DfES, 2005, p. 7)

The guidance makes it clear that the difficulties of vulnerable children should be addressed as part of an overall school approach:

> Supplementary materials are provided in the pack for children who may need additional help in small groups, but the main focus is on a universal entitlement to school-based social and emotional learning for *all* children. (DfES, 2005, p. 14)

Teachers can enable these children to cope with the injustice they face in the short term, acknowledge the unfairness, and move on without being damaged in the long term. Children can make sense of what happens to them and forgive those individuals involved provided that teachers are aware of their feelings. However, this should be part of a wider initiative of school change, and teachers need to see emotional development as part of overall child development and learning:

> Or they may be promoting children's development through other initiatives such as circle time, self-esteem approaches, peer mediation, and commercially available schemes that specifically teach social, emotional and behavioural skills. In addition many schools and settings provide extra support for children whose behavioural, social or emotional development is of concern. (DfES, 2005, p. 10)

So, with attention to personal feelings in mind, teachers need urgently to become proactive (rather than reactive) on issues of emotional wellbeing in the classroom, as Geddes explains, in relation to directives that are driven by measures of performance and achievement:

> It is worrying to note that often this is expressed in schools as division of responsibility; between learning and welfare – between cognition and emotion – between practice and process. . . . Schools can 'make a difference' and do have the potential to be emotionally and mentally healthy institutions when the match between educational goals and pupil developmental and emotional needs can coincide. (Geddes, 2006, p. 139)

Unfortunately, that very division of responsibility has a negative effect on practice. This is especially true when the individual child's personal needs and priorities are marginalized in favour of academic or remedial activity. Separating the cognitive from the emotional means that behaviours associated with strong feelings are often treated as a cause when in fact they are symptoms.

To ignore the relationship between cognitive and emotional responses can be highly detrimental to effective learning, yet successful practice shows that providing choices of task, learning processes and different levels of participation improve behaviour and sociability for all young people, not just those in the most challenging of circumstances. Strategies such as peer support and co-mentoring allow positive reflection and the development of proactive strategies that improve relationships and tackle the causes of difficult behaviour.

The issues of support and intervention are often contentious, particularly when limited resources must be shared. In schools where teachers and school leaders do not recognize the inequalities that prevail, it is generally assumed that resources should be distributed hierarchically – that is, favouring the most academically able. This is reflected across the whole education system. The evidence is that investment in the early years has the greatest impact on life chances and wellbeing, yet funding remains stubbornly age related. If the per capita spending in post-compulsory education were to be replicated in the early years, then we would see one of the greatest educational revolutions in modern history. The sustained discrimination favouring the older and most able is what Beck and Stanovich (2000) described as the 'Matthew Effect': in essence, Matthew's Gospel (25:29) appears to claim that the rich will get richer and the poor get poorer. The problem is that, without basic skill acquisition, higher order skills become increasingly hard to master.

If a child learns to read easily, he or she is likely to continue to do well more quickly: having mastered reading he or she will be able to access wider and more complex learning. In contrast, the child with initial difficulties will not only struggle from the start but, without extra help, will have to work increasingly hard to catch up. Inevitably, such prejudice impacts on self-esteem, inhibits participation and reduces the effort children put into learning. When they are expected only to achieve a minimum level of achievement, when aspirations and expectations are low, vulnerable children are more likely to give up quickly and may thus lose the support that would help them to participate. Taking the contrary view, opening up more resources for those that need them – and are therefore entitled to them – will have a positive impact on the whole school, college or university, as it articulates a belief in achievement through *effort* rather than apparent ability. At the same time, lower sets and bands reinforce a belief in fixed ability that reduces children's inclination to overcome their additional barriers. Being able to provide the extra support required will help motivate vulnerable children, increase their skill development and enable them to break the negative cycle.

School cultures that only reward high academic achievement will ultimately have a negative effect on the motivation and engagement of *all* children: it is not only vulnerable children who lose, but the whole educational community:

> I once was a math whiz. In high school, I got a 99 in algebra, a 99 in geometry, and a 99 in trigonometry, and I was on the math team.
> Then I got a Mr Hellman, a teacher who didn't believe girls could do math. My grades declined, and I never took math again. (Dweck, 2006, p. 74)

Different performance expectations for different children (whether they are perceived as gifted or deficient) reinforce unfairness in treatment and opportunity, and stifle encouragement of effort. Vulnerable children may be trying hardest already, but the message they receive in a performance culture is harsh and repressive.

By classifying subjects into areas that are perceived as 'more' or 'less' useful, schools add to the pressures of inequality. The unconscious prejudice of some people in education to reward result over effort, reinforced by sets and banding, puts a cap on perceived potential. In practice, individuals are treated unfairly because of expectations determined by their background, gender and impairments:

... systems which identify academic success as the only hallmark of education success are potentially very damaging. Times have certainly changed and there is greater equality of opportunity implied in current practice. However, the hysteria produced by starred A level results can feel very disheartening to vulnerable pupils whose academic needs and capacities are not recognised with the same degree of interest. ... humiliation can be a trigger for powerful defensive behaviours, involving anger and disaffection. (Geddes, 2006, p. 61)

If young people receive help and support in equal measure, vulnerable children who need most help will be denied more typical opportunities that others take for granted.

As we have established, ensuring every child's wellbeing by addressing inequality within the system cannot be done fairly without the urgent direction of greater resources for those in most need. The issue of fairness is both complex and sensitive and requires clear explanation and careful handling, so that all parties understand the reasons for change. As Lumby with Coleman (2007) explain, if participants do not understand the need to prioritize help to certain groups, resentment occurs. Being unclear about inequality, and failing to clarify change, leaves participants wondering why resources are going to those perceived as needy.

The social weighting of opportunity needs clearer articulation and shared commitment. Furthermore, it must be acknowledged throughout early years' settings, schools, colleges and universities that simultaneous action has to be taken on many levels. Otherwise, the system will probably continue to favour achievement. Clarity of reason and purpose must be adopted across organizations, with advances in knowledge and practice leading attitudinal and cultural change. A change in culture is particularly important in order to effect real and long-term changes in practice:

> What the relationship with inequality actually demonstrates is that societies that tolerate the injustices of great inequality will almost always inescapably suffer their social consequences: they will be unfriendly and violent societies recognised more for their hostility than for their hospitality. (Wilkinson, 2005, p. 36)

All too often, understanding the need to change one's practice translates poorly into action. The education system often confounds equality by embracing hierarchy in everyday practice. For example, while establishing a university equality scheme, a photograph of a black student with learning difficulties was placed in the 'Disability' section in the university prospectus. Rather than clarifying, this confuses issues of differentiation, access and equal opportunities to learning. Despite the scheme, nobody has thought to depict disabled students as equals: they are still perceived in practice as having *other* needs that are the responsibility of the *Disability Support Services*.

Such acts are rarely described in terms of discrimination and might seem inconsequential, but they point to a profound lack of understanding of student equality in action. In all probability, they are kind and caring people who have good reasons and valid motives for their actions.

It is now widely understood from a range of perspectives that relationships with significant adults in the early years are of pivotal importance. For some vulnerable children, the early years setting or the school may provide the only secure base in their lives. Factors affecting vulnerable children outside the school (e.g. being 'looked after', the family's capacity to cope with break-up, loss, unemployment, or the impact of physical or cultural difference) may mean that children come into school with a specific need for attachment. Such children's ability to cope will then depend greatly on their relationships at school. As Keverne puts it:

> Awareness of the sensitive phases in brain development is important to understanding how we might facilitate secure relationships and high self-esteem in our children. This will provide the firm foundations on which to develop meaningful lifestyles and relationships that are crucial to adult wellbeing. (Huppert et al., 2005, p. 35)

Geddes (2006) takes an Attachment Theory perspective to supporting child development through secure relationships. She explains that, without the support of early intervention, social and emotional experience can interact and lead to difficult behaviour in the classroom unless teachers seek to understand it and respond appropriately. She explains:

> For children of insecure attachment experience, adversity can be meliorated by relationships with other significant carers. Fathers, siblings, grandparents, relatives and friends can offer more positive experiences which will enhance esteem and resilience. In this way political climate and community also contribute to overall wellbeing of children. (Geddes, 2006, p. 63)

Strategies that support relationships will have both immediate and long-term impact on their wellbeing from childhood into adulthood. Initiatives such as toddler groups, family days and fathers' breakfast groups all have a pivotal role to play in strengthening relationships, and therefore enrich the child's development.

Later in school life, young people need to have good opportunities to make friends. Friendships are valuable not only socially but in terms of protecting a child and helping him or her to become more resilient during puberty and other times of particular stress:

> Puberty is a vulnerable period for the development of numerous problems including eating disorders, obsessive compulsive disorders, addictive disorders, onset of depression, and in some cases suicide ... In adolescents, identity formation and self-esteem are central issues in psychological development, and having more than four close friends seems to be protective against the development of depressive symptoms.
>
> ... on the basis of secure attachment, the extended period from infancy to puberty, longer for humans than for any primate, has enabled the expansion of social relationships that provided a buffer for regulating the emotional turmoil of puberty. (Huppert et al., 2005, pp. 42–4)

In the long term, converting this understanding into practice will reinforce safety and security in periods of higher stress. Understanding the link between relationships and positive self-image emphasizes the need to encourage positive, nurturing cultures that place relationships first and targets second. Most importantly for wellbeing, Geddes explains how early relationships with teachers and parents lay out the dynamics of later life:

> In this way it is possible to think of engagement in learning, in the educational task, as a precursor to engagement in work and social life. The capacity to access opportunity in terms of social inclusion may have its roots in the same experiences which can inhibit learning – attachment relationships. (Geddes, 2006, p. 63)

Early years practitioners are particularly good at recognizing age and stage – they focus on the relative level of a child's development rather than their chronological level. However as young people move through primary and secondary education, performance-focused practice can have an increasingly negative impact on young people's relationships; automatic chronological cohort progression (i.e. the movement from one year to another irrespective of readiness or maturity) reinforces and demonstrates on a daily basis systemic inequality where the coherence of the system is more important than the integrity of the personal experience. Where practice bars the support of friends, it adds to the isolation of those who feel marginalized in the first place. As a result, the effort required to keep up and flourish will inevitably be far greater for vulnerable children:

> People have different resources and opportunities. For example, people with money (or rich parents) have a safety net. They can take more risks and keep going longer until they succeed. People with easy access to good education, people with a network of influential friends, people who know how to be in the right place at the right time – all stand a better chance of having heir effort paid off. Rich, educated,

connected effort works better. People with fewer resources, in spite of their best efforts, can be derailed more easily. (Dweck, 2006, p. 47)

We shall look later in more detail at the issue of effort, but since all children are capable of equal effort it is key to redressing inequality. Even if results vary, valuing effort unlocks possibilities for hope and aspirations in a way that targets do not. While education cannot solve poverty, schools can make a long-term difference by supplying the factors for success: engagement in learning and community connection in the form of meaningful relationships. These factors increase the likelihood of sustained effort and long-term success. Without them, vulnerable children may be 'derailed'.

The wellbeing of vulnerable children remains threatened as long as educators fail to differentiate in their practice between systems and relationships. The perception of equality as a minority issue is fundamentally harmful, as it places blame on the most vulnerable by implying individual responsibility for failure. This deficit perspective skews teachers' and practitioners' understanding of the impact of inequality. Clear articulation and remedy are critical for the welfare of vulnerable children. Only by reducing discrimination in practice in the short term will early years' settings, schools, colleges and universities be effective in increasing chances of long-term success.

Schools can make a difference by:

- clearly expressing inequality as an outcome of an unfair system
- being proactive and sharing strategies that tackle the impact of stereotypes on effort and performance
- challenging the everyday practice that leads to prejudice and discrimination
- explaining that bullying happens as a result of social factors that impact on children beyond the playground
- supporting relationships, thus developing the resilience children need to deal with discrimination.

5 Health and balance

This chapter offers a offer a positive definition for health within a wider concept of wellbeing. This keystone concept enables us to develop ideas and build a model of wellbeing in which children can flourish. We begin by examining social aspects of health and identify how they impact on the individual. Later, we outline the personal aspects and explore the choices that are so critical to illness prevention.

Because deficit, negative and exceptional models are so deeply entrenched in society's collective psyche, a positive definition of health is hard to grasp. This explains why, on the one hand, 'lack of health' has been seen as a personal misfortune; the pain and suffering of the few is the responsibility of the specialist in care and cure. On the other hand, it also explains why the wider population identifies good health as the specific remit of the medical profession; their job is to keep us all healthy. The division between those perceived as 'healthy' and 'unhealthy' has led to a concept of health biased towards find-and-fix, or a medical model based on cure. The prevailing health service culture is based on providing remedies and curing disease: it operates from a perspective of reaction rather than prevention and intervention.

It is easy to see why some medical approaches blame the most vulnerable for their illness (which then becomes a self-fulfilling prophecy), given their low status in society. If in the public mind those in need are cared for with a separate pot of money, they are easily perceived as *responsible* for poverty rather than as its victims. Inequalities become most deeply entrenched when those deprived of the factors supporting resilience turn to quick fixes: this deepens prejudice and excuses criticism. While poverty of opportunity does increase the likelihood of ill health, studies have shown that mental illness is seen a much bigger problem in terms of wellbeing. However, mental illness and addiction are perceived as less significant despite the fact that a third of the population experience these problems at some point in their lives. In the case of serious mental illness (which 15 per cent of the population will experience in severe or physiologically impairing form) the cost of treatment is small relative to the huge improvements in wellbeing. Yet the majority of people will be given no treatment at all and mental illness receives only 13 per cent of the health budget, with 5 per cent spent on research (Layard, 2005).

The greatest challenge facing all services is the paradigm shift from operational crisis management to strategic intervention and long-term progression. Health has traditionally been seen as the remit of remedial experts, GPs and specialists who are called upon when things go wrong. Consequently there is a strong risk that health issues are perceived as divorced from education, or, worse still, form the remit of other agencies. In such cases tragedies occur, as highlighted by the child abuse cases in Haringey and Doncaster in 2008. The importance of cohesive, preventative action to ensure children's wellbeing has rarely been so high on every agenda, and education has a major role to play. The *Guidance for Schools on Promoting Pupil Wellbeing* summarizes this:

> ... it does not mean that schools can focus only on educational outcomes, narrowly defined. All the *Every Child Matters* outcomes are intrinsic to an individual child's development. They are all important in their own right and they are also mutually reinforcing: children in poor health or who do not feel safe will not be able to learn effectively; conversely doing well in class can boost children's self-esteem and their emotional resilience. (p. 9)

With the fifth principle of *The Children's Plan* (DCSF, 2007b) in mind, 'it is always better to prevent failure than tackle a crisis later', the next section starts by examining the principles that underpin prevention. If wellbeing is addressed in schools, it will contribute significantly to children's enduring health:

> The link between educational standards and the wellbeing of children and young people is well proven and PSHE [personal, social and health education] offers a significant route to strengthening this relationship. (NHS/DCSF, 2008, p. 5)

These views are rarely challenged but have a profound influence on culture. In addition, health research has been heavily motivated by post-war problems that have needed cures and solutions. The success of science in alleviating human suffering has been tremendous. However it has failed to increase wellbeing across the whole of society. Essentially, the qualities shared by those who flourish are very different from states of moderate satisfaction. If identified and shared, their benefits would substantially improve health for entire communities.

A thriving population demands not only illness prevention but a proactive understanding of health. Success should be viewed as an outcome of *health enhancement*, through which wellbeing can benefit whole populations.

> Controlled trials have shown that well-designed courses in emotional-intelligence have significant effects on children's mood and on their consideration for others; these effects are still evident two years later. Since all children benefit from acquiring inner strength, some of these courses have been aimed at all children. (Layard, 2005, p. 200)

Schools need to pay greater attention to enabling children to flourish. PSHE is presently given one hour a week, so its impact on physical and mental wealth is limited. However, the potential for schools to deliver on enhancing health is immense. It requires greater attention to the key factors that enable young people to thrive. Education needs to grasp the positive social and psychological benefits linked with health. It needs to adopt clear strategies to promote these ideas and teach the basic knowledge that supports healthy lifestyles. Provided that they base their strategies on positive models, schools have the power to foster flourishing in the short term and wellbeing in the long term. The ideas emerge from recent research on subjective wellbeing and they are supported by new theories from the field of positive psychology. Our initial perspective is chosen quite specifically to deal with specific threats to young people's health: diet and television. Recent evidence suggests these have an overwhelming negative effect on physical and mental health because they threaten both personal balance and engagement.

Like any other aspect of wellbeing, children's health needs early intervention for positive impact and long-term benefits. From a safety-and-health perspective, schools, colleges and universities have a duty to safeguard young people and staff from harm and injury. Wellbeing demands action at a deeper level, simultaneously addressing those issues within the system that first pose a threat to health and promoting ideas and skills that enhance it.

In their book on school sustainability, Hargreaves and Fink (2005) refer to the elements that contribute to sustainable schools as a 'meal not a menu'. In the same way, children need every course (including the pudding!). However, the quantities of each will vary according to need. None are dispensable or more singularly important, as each carries quite specific qualities that others do not have. This idea is critical: in essence what sustains children's health is their strength and the factors that contribute the strength are wide and varied. Without sufficient courses to sustain it, the organism loses integrity and the whole collapses. To prevent collapse, balance must remain a focus.

Defining physical and mental wealth

Health and wellbeing are frequently confused, and the words are often used synonymously. However, reducing the former to a narrow definition of the latter diminishes any appreciation of health and wellbeing as all-embracing, long term, and influencing every aspect of children's lives. While being free from hurt and pain is definitely the best starting point, it falls short of *flourishing*, which necessitates a wealth of positive factors both personal and social.

For the purpose of education, health is best defined as the personal capacity that enables an individual to flourish in any situation. This goes further than the idea of health as the absence of pain, lack of suffering caused by illness, good physical and emotional working order within a narrow and present timeframe. It means having everything needed to engage in the day-to-day activity of being on every level – physical, emotional and spiritual. This perspective is reflected in *The Children's Plan*:

> Good health is vital if children and young people are to enjoy their childhood and achieve their full potential. If we can establish good habits in childhood, this will provide the basis for lifelong health and wellbeing. (DCSF, 2007b, p. 9)

Without good health, children are in crisis. However, some inconsequential habits in young people's lives can become critical for long-term wellbeing. It is like navigating a super-tanker: to ensure everything runs smoothly, action is taken hours before the results are observed. Although little harm is immediately apparent when the tanker veers off-course, damage will occur and getting back on-course again may be time-consuming and costly. Keeping the vessel on course is far preferable but only achievable if the long-term target is kept in view.

Understanding health in these terms is closer to ancient models based on interaction and interconnectedness. For shamans or traditional healers, health is a holistic concept that embraces physical health as well as emotional and spiritual wellbeing. The human connection to greater systems (e.g. the environment and the earth) and greater spiritual oneness (irrespective of deity or religion) delivers wellbeing. Ill health was seen to emanate from a disruption in the relationship between these factors and physical, emotional or spiritual balance. In the following sections we seek to re-establish the beneficial relationships so that children can thrive by exploring what currently favours and threatens this ecology of body and spirit.

In accordance with wellbeing theory, a contemporary definition of health needs to address both emotional and physical fitness in the short term as well as setting up the right conditions for continued flourishing in the long term. If we can prevent the stress caused by imbalance, and nurture full engagement in positive activities, we should be able to improve every child's opportunity to be healthy and flourish.

The need for a more balanced approach to lifestyle is reflected in current social concerns. Teachers and practitioners don't have to become nutritionists, but they are in an ideal position to give children the knowledge they need to make healthy choices. With this in mind, they need urgently to understand the impact of diet on both physical and social wellbeing. Physically and emotionally strong young people are able to learn, fully engage in school life and stand strong in the face of pressures and adversity. The government describes its Healthy Schools Programme as: 'An exciting long-term initiative that promotes the link between good health, behaviour and achievement.'

Balance and extremes

Before identifying the factors that contribute to health in terms of personal wealth, it is helpful to identify the wider social pressures that create imbalance in young people's lives. Those pressures (some created by the organization of education) influence choice and impose norms that hinder wellbeing. Understanding what causes inequality reduces the feeling of powerlessness in decision-making and increases the ability to make the right choice even when the options are limited. Food is a helpful example in this context since it is the 'meeting point of social and physical world', it is central to all life and essential to life irrespective of race, age, income, social class, ability or legislative boundary (Gesch, cited in Huppert et al., 2005).

The causes of social imbalance are far-reaching. However, its outcomes for different communities are clear and well defined. Differences across populations are striking: both nationally and globally, whole communities are fragmented by polarized extremes. The impact on health is pronounced, for lack of access to shared resources leads to illness and early death. This imbalance – an acceptance of unfairness – demonstrates a profound lack of understanding of social justice. The patterns are clear:

> It does not have to be this way and it is not right that it should be like this. Where systematic differences in health are judged to be avoidable by reasonable action they are, quite simply, unfair. It is this that we label health inequity ... Reducing health inequities is ... an ethical imperative. Social injustice is killing people on a grand scale. (WHO, 2008, p. 4)

Uneven distribution means that only certain communities within the population can access a complete menu for flourishing. While some squander limited resources, the imbalance is highly detrimental to certain social groups. At the national table very few can indulge in a full selection of courses – the full choice of culinary delights that delivers sufficient variety for nutritional balance. The excesses are far from healthy: where resources are plentiful, diets are over-processed and high in refined carbohydrate and fat which can cause obesity, mental illness and aggression. At the other extreme, for those with less privileged socio-economic positions, poor education and poverty seriously affect life outcomes. Across the population, lack of knowledge about what a healthy meal looks like and insufficient training in healthy habits affects the wellbeing of different communities in different ways. Extreme positions can prove fatal:

> Early child development (ECD) – including the physical, social/emotional, and language/cognitive domains – has a determining influence on subsequent life chances and health through skills development, education, and occupational opportunities. Through these mechanisms and directly, early childhood influences subsequent risk of obesity, malnutrition, mental health problems, heart disease, and criminality ... This has huge implications for their health and for society at large. Children need safe, healthy, supporting, nurturing, caring, and responsive living environments. (WHO, 2008, p. 6)

Aggravated by modern social trends, the imbalance is deepening as factors affecting extremes remain unaltered and wellbeing is hindered across the board. Ultimately, the problems born of this continuing cycle of imbalance and deprivation will negatively affect the whole population:

> With the onset of industrialization from around 200 years ago, it seems from the perspective of what we eat that a miracle must have occurred, because irrespective of how much salt, saturated fat, hydrogenated fats, and refined sugar we started eating we seemed to assume it had no implications for our well-being. (Gesh et al., cited in Huppert et al., 2005, p. 176)

Young people's physical health is jeopardized by increasingly individualist, 'grab-and-go' habits and by the resulting poor diets. Mental health is also at risk as the beneficial aspects of social mealtime habits are lost at great expense to wellbeing.

Food inequality is a major cause of malnutrition, leading to hunger and severe dietary imbalance. A more disturbing aspect seems to be the effect of high-fat high-energy diets on the brain: patterns of mental illness including depression and schizophrenia also follow the nutritional excess and imbalance associated with modern dietary practice (Gesch cited in Huppert et al., 2005).

> Evidence is emerging that diet may be linked with childhood development disorders. Many of the features associated with attention deficit hyperactivity disorder (ADHD), dyslexia, dyspraxia, and autistic spectrum disorders are consistent with a lack of or imbalance in highly unsaturated fatty acids. (Huppert et al., 2005, p. 184)

The link between diet and behaviour is now more widely recognized: from a wellbeing perspective it forms the thick end of a worrying wedge, but it should be approached with caution. However, the evidence is convincing, and it helps us to recognize that poor dietary balance can affect children's behaviour. Furthermore, what may have a limited impact on most children could actually cause problems for others. Evidence suggests that diet affects children's moods, particularly for those who lack the basic level of nutrition to maintain good health. Increasing the variety of natural, unprocessed foods is likely to improve behaviour across the board. If (as evidence suggests) diet and aggressive tendencies are linked, then addressing the cause of poor diet will reduce bullying. Gesch's evidence on the effects of poor diet and criminality are compelling. His assertion of a link between poor diet and aggressive behaviour in prison populations is supported by hard evidence. Data show rapid and positive behavioural outcomes from a balanced diet and nutrition education.

In relation to education this seems to support Jamie Oliver's enthusiastic (if ill-received) ideas that knowledge is key to improving the British diet. The idea that people no longer have survival skills is clearly a matter that the education system can address. Oliver is quoted as having discovered a new form of poverty caused by people with 'a massive lack of knowledge' and short of the basic life skills they need to feed their own families. One mother he filmed had never made a home-cooked meal for her five-year-old daughter and another did not know that water bubbles when it boils.

In a standards culture that is overly concerned with purely academic targets, the longstanding hierarchy of school subjects has resulted in reduced opportunities to learn essential life skills. There will come a point where education will have to ask whether increasing attainment levels have any relevance in a nation the citizens of which can no longer feed themselves. Perhaps there is a greater urgency for all learners to more thoroughly explore dietary knowledge beyond the academic: knowing what 'a balanced diet' means and putting it into practice are quite different. Reading a recipe or watching a cookery programme can never replace the physical and spatial understanding involved in preparing and delivering the different dishes that make up a balanced meal.

New research and awareness is pivotal in addressing the causes of poor diet. In addition, it is far more constructive to increase skills and knowledge than to condemn children for the behaviour caused by lacking them. 'In doing so we may need to choose if we prefer to lock up ever more of our nation's children or to nourish them properly' (Gesch, cited in Huppert et al., 2005). Ultimately, we need to reassess dietary standards to take account of mental health, developmental, behavioural and cognitive parameters:

> We need to develop our understanding of the dosage and range of nutrients required to positively impact the human condition. It may be a recipe that goes beyond individual well-being; it may be a recipe for peace. (Huppert et al., 2005, p. 201)

The benefits of a varied diet have recently been much publicised as essential to good health. Such benefits include both the range of nutrients needed to support the human body as a functioning system and the satisfaction of being able to enjoy a choice of dishes that satisfy our appetites for choice. Campaigns, such as '5-a-day', 'Just Eat More (fruit and veg)' and 'Rainbow Food', have given clear messages about the benefits of dietary diversity. The 'eatwell plate' clearly gives a different message with significant visual impact. It supports current understanding and encourages a more varied approach to dietary balance. The Food Standards Agency states: 'Placing emphasis on "getting the balance right" was found to reinforce the main healthy eating message and came across as dynamic, instilling confidence and suggesting that everyone can do it.'

The problem with the post-industrial diet is not so much about long-term harm. Most will survive on a poor diet but, because the human appetite is finite, the more we eat of the same foodstuff the less room we have for essential variety that supplies the range of nutrients we require. Some trace nutrients are derived only when diet is broad as well as balanced. What's more, these small quantities essential to child growth are most likely to be absent in convenience food. We need to help children to understand what constitutes an adequate range, so that they can understand the benefits and make choices. In experiments on the effect on cognition of zinc intake, the supplement level required to lift an individual from baseline to optimum is tiny; large increases have little added effect.

Personal taste comes into play here: taste can often mislead with unfortunate consequences, most notably when people's ability 'want' things that they do not necessarily even 'like' (Gilbert, 2005). Research shows that people often carry on wanting (particularly addictive substances) long after their liking or desire has been satisfied. In other words, what people like and what they want are affected by subconscious psychological drives which can create conflict rather than satisfaction.

Unless people understand these urges, they might eat only what they 'want' at great cost to the health, as their nutritional range narrows and skews. Unless children are taught about these differences, they are likely to make decisions about what they eat based on their misleading feelings and understanding.

More often than not, a healthy meal will provide as much pleasure, despite its limited initial attraction: wise are those who can make the right decision and satisfy both urge and pleasure. However, to achieve this wisdom children need to have the information and be encouraged to develop the understanding of the differences outlined in the previous paragraph. Also, more crucially, they need to know how to apply this to their eating habits. If children appreciate that their feelings towards food may be misguided, they might be more ready to try different things. Eventually this will help improve wellbeing, as the skills necessary for healthy eating apply also to other areas such as considering other perspectives, long-term choice implications and cognitive led self-control.

The concept of individual integrity is helpful here as it offers a positive model for maintaining and increasing the strength of the human system by choice. It incorporates the wider implications explored above, with regard to balance and breadth, and applies them to the long term, making further growth possible and increasing resilience through sustainable action. Integrity fits better with a proactive model of flourishing, whereas other ideas explaining resilience tend to focus on children's reaction to events. Integrity, on the other hand, implies taking positive decisions led by control and responsibility for future health. Thus, wellbeing is achieved not by reacting to chance, but by deliberate intent and mindful of existing pressure.

From this perspective, meeting the physical, emotional and spiritual needs of all involved creates synergy. For example, a child whose physical health is strong is still prone to infection if his or her emotional health is neglected. In this way, lack of confidence will in time become low self-esteem, provoking sadness or depression for which physical strength cannot compensate. Similarly, a group of children deprived of 60 minutes physical activity per day will miss out on opportunities to develop strength and possibly risk mental illness.

Increasing concerns about obesity and antisocial behaviour are reflected daily in the media and priorities have been clarified across all government agencies:

> The whole school approach involves working with children and young people, parents, school staff and the whole school community to provide a solid foundation from which developments and improvement are embedded in a systematic way. These processes contribute to the physical and emotional development of all members of the school community. (Healthy Schools, 2009)

Everyone needs to consider the factors that affect and influence their integrity, and it needs to be made very clear that developing personal integrity is by no means a remedy for specific problems. Every child requires integrity, although strength may be enhanced using many different strategies. Our ideas here are intended to inform more generally on the principle that all young people should be given the key skills and understanding that offer an equal opportunity to flourish.

Optimum and maximum

The issue of organism integrity and overall capacity demands careful consideration when dividing finite resources. Focusing unduly on any one aspect automatically detracts from other aspects. Given the limited (if essential) role of health in overall wellbeing, an over-concentration on eating habits in the long run would be detrimental to overall wellbeing. Health, like wellbeing, encompasses many other aspects. Therefore eating healthily must not exclude outcomes such as safety, happiness or relationships. More fundamentally, seeking to achieve maximum outcomes in any one area could significantly reduce the chances of more general fulfilment. As Layard explains, with regard to happiness:

> One gets some idea of the strain of optimising by comparing the happiness of 'maximisers' (who seek the best) and 'satisfisers' (who are content with what is good enough). (Layard, 2005, p. 198)

While achieving satisfaction might be perceived as falling short of government standards, achieving improvement exclusively in the top percentile can only happen at a cost. If excellence is understood in exclusive terms it will threaten overall integrity, i.e. optimum results for all learners. Sadly, guidance aimed at improving result scores of a top percentile will have a detrimental effect on the majority. So the pursuit of excellence needs to be defined as the majority achieving above an average level, to a satisfactory and broad level, and not to a maximum level.

In very real ways, the education system's pursuit of higher test results is a perfect example of the maximizing culture that leads to imbalance and diminishing returns. We are not denying that standards should be addressed. But at what cost? If the boundaries within which the standards are measured are too narrow and too prescriptive, the likelihood is that the lack of breadth needed for integrity will threaten the achievement of potential for every child

Education has concentrated heavily on the replication of information and linguistic and logical skills at the expense of the physical and emotional development necessary for wellbeing. In consequence, the broad range of skills needed for baseline wellbeing has been neglected, creating an imbalance and lack of resilience among young people. This neglect is most acutely felt by those who suffer as a consequence of this impoverishment, for example children who develop mental difficulties as a result of diminishing opportunity to develop the skills underlying better health. Unfortunately, attempting to repair neglect later on is in the context of child wellbeing akin to 'adding the eggs after you've baked the cake' (Robinson, 2005).

6 Physical activity and emotional health

Introduction

In the last chapter we looked at some basic principles underpinning children's physical health; in this chapter we turn to ideas that have a positive impact on their emotional lives. Many of the factors that threaten young people's health are social and intrinsically linked to modern-day living. Contemporary consumer lifestyles with their strong emphasis on material affluence create an imbalance in that permeates the education system. Individualism is now perceived as a societal *right*; satisfying the urge for material wealth takes precedence over more gratifying pleasures such as social interaction and physical activity. Passive and isolating activity (such as watching television) and a lack of proactive understanding around mental health further compound the negative factors in children's lives. Dealing with these pressures also renders children less able to find satisfaction in real life or the present moment. Positive factors need attention if schools are to deliver on the third principle of *The Children's Plan* (DCSF, 2007b), which states: 'children and young people need to enjoy their childhood as well as grow up prepared for adult life'.

Unfortunately, modern lifestyles characterized by financial gain and squandered resources reduce the likelihood of a happy experience of childhood. In addition, there is a growing sense that childhood itself is threatened by society's prejudiced views of children and ambivalence towards their status. This is characterized by negative attitudes to other people's children, and the idea that, as 'not yet adults', children deserve only restricted 'rights' until they can fully contribute to economic production. These dissonant views make it hard to identify the factors within current practice that protect and enhance wellbeing, and the further development of strategies to those ends.

As the 'Good Childhood Report' identifies, the consumerism that characterizes adult lives imposes norms and expectations that are oppressive to children. From the perspective of educational purpose, this is an attitude that may need to be addressed through an increased focus on collaboration and search for personal responsibility in achieving the common good. The Children's Society Report calls for 'a radical shift away from the excessively individualistic ethos':

> Some looked to consumerism to explain current levels of mental health problems amongst children. 'Some commentators believe that the rampant materialism of our consumer society fuelled by television advertising – much of which is directed to children and young people – is damaging their emotional well-being, particularly in the case of those on low incomes, contributing to worryingly high levels of depression and mental health problems. (Layard and Dunn, 2009, p. 8)

'Relationship with Reality' theory argues that the thoughts and actions adopted to cope with these pressures actually cause many health problems. Egotistical behaviour has a negative impact on children by imposing distorted views of reality. While diets impact on mood, the perception of low status aggravated by materialism and consumerism further contributes to problems such as depression, obesity, drinking and drug abuse.

According to Baylis (Huppert et al., 2005), Relationship with Reality theory attempts to explain the motivation behind thoughts and actions that make up a personal style for dealing with real life. He explains that children's imagination and future achievement depend critically on making the distinction between positive *dreaming* and negative *fantasy*. Through this lens, children's thoughts and actions can be seen as mixture of reality-investing, quick-fixing and reality-evading thoughts and actions. How young people use these to develop their own coping strategies will determine how much they engage with real life. In the long term their overall approach to life will be a deciding factor in their emotional health. Enabling children to develop increasingly reality-investing thoughts and actions will help add to the positive factors contributing to their wellbeing. This will also enable them to make better choices regarding the types of behaviour that have long-term impact on their own health.

Layard identifies television as one of the major factors contributing to people's general unhappiness and a rise in mental difficulties. Television tends to stimulate social comparison, thus contributing to the stress in children's lives. Watching hours of enhanced living is detrimental to young people's self-image and therefore to their emotional health:

> Young people themselves highlighted the importance of being free from stress, pressure and worry. (Layard and Dunn, 2009, p. 3)

Physical activity, on the other hand, provides an alternative activity which counters both isolation and passivity directly. As the research into its psychological effects demonstrate:

> ... reviews have generally concluded that physical activity is associated with reduced anxiety, reduced depression, improved mood states, enhanced health-related quality of life in the elderly and various patient populations, improved physical and general self-worth, improved sleep, reduced reactivity to psychological stressors and improved cognitive function in all populations including older adults.
> (Huppert et al., 2006, p. 145)

Providing more opportunities for young people to engage in all types of physical activity is therefore important because the resulting positive factors are both dynamic and immediate. Physical activity not only provides opportunities for developing a broader intelligence, but it also helps build the social relationships and physical awareness that are so beneficial to emotional wealth and stress reduction.

These ideas should provide a sound basis for strategies designed to motivate a more healthy engagement with reality, with long-term implications for wellbeing. In terms of the emphasis within *The Children's Plan* (DCSF, 2007b) regarding staying on track and achieving post-18 potential, it is essential to address the issues that prevent disengagement. Behind the addictive behaviour and 'quick-fix' solutions that arise when young people disengage, lie more deeply set social isolation issues and the increasing stresses of coping with real life (Huppert et al., 2005).

Baylis outlines three categories to define different motivation found in young people's attitude to life. From these he identified the different patterns in the strategies children use to achieve less pain or more pleasure. The first category is 'reality-evading', strategies employed include using escapist fantasy, television or drug abuse to avoid pain or challenge. The second is 'quick-fixing', which, for example, could involve lying, exaggeration or using comfort food or alcohol in order to bring temporary relief from pain or anxiety. The third is 'reality-investing', which, for example, includes planning, practising or seeking mentorship in order to improve real-life experience. Young people's *relationship with reality* is determined by the relative use of different aims and strategies, and the final balance determines a child's distinctive personality. The impact on wellbeing of a child's relationship with reality and how much they invest, quick-fix or evade real life, will prove either helpful or harmful over time and will affect their emotional wealth accordingly.

Consumerism and individualism

With its remarkable leaps in technological development, twenty-first century living carries negative side effects that can distort young people's sense of reality and damage their mental health (Huppert et al., 2005). Technology empowers and liberates in many ways, particularly in establishing contact and closeness in relationships. Technological advances mean that communities now extend globally and are no longer defined by background or geographical proximity. However, the negative aspect of this revolution is the distortion created by digital communication, which reduces face-to-face interaction and may impair the social habits that underpin social intelligence.

> 44% of British children who use the internet say they have made friends online, compared with 32% in France. (Grimston, 2009)

The isolation caused by the virtual world can alter both mood and perception, and affect young people's relationships. Relationships that exist without physical presence are prone to fantasy and may be built on lies and self-denial; they may arise from wants and desires that also reduce the possibility of satisfying their need for closeness. While the medium per se is not to blame, its use can provoke reality-evading thoughts and actions. Like other addictions, this is detrimental to long-term physical and mental health. One remarkable aspect of the technological revolution is the proliferation of television sets in young people's homes. In 1950 there were very few televisions: families often shared them and watching television was a social activity bringing people together. By 1960 they were commonplace in many homes and no doubt every person in the industrialized world will soon own one (Layard, 2005).

The progression from shared activity to individual experience is typical of consumerism and the egocentric attitudes that underpin a 'must-have' mindset. These offer justification for giving in to the 'wanting' urges that create imbalance and stress in the long run (see Chapter 4). Watching television might satisfy a need for escapism, but it prevents people from the reality-investing thoughts and actions such as sharing common interests. On a deeper level it backs an individualistic view with the acceptance that to own a television is a *right*, and that making life better for oneself has no impact on others.

Not only has watching television become an increasingly isolating activity that reduces social interaction, but also viewing time itself has a cost. Research shows that watching television reduces social and physical activity, thus reducing opportunity for relationships and creativity (Layard, 2005). Spending more time passively viewing has cognitive-behavioural implications that are directly detrimental to child development. Images that glamorize celebrity, encourage continuous and high-activity pursuits, and desensitize viewers to crime and violence, will affect children's expectations, thoughts and actions.

While the medium of television is not necessarily a problem, the lives it depicts, enhanced for entertainment purposes, have a negative impact on children's perception of reality. Programmes that show high activity, violence and extremes of emotion do not reflect daily life, but set expectation beyond ordinary boundaries. These unrealistic comparisons stimulate stress and hopelessness:

> Mental health problems were considered to be associated with material deprivation. 'Poverty and deprivation give rise to feelings of hopelessness, despair, frustration, anger and low self worth. This, in turn, affects relationships, the quality of care of children and how people care for themselves. (Layard and Dunn, 2009, p. 8)

Whether they show beautiful people with unrealistic wares or 'reality television' that plays on stereotypes by highlighting difficult behaviour or deprivation. Television fuels the prejudice that generates feelings of inferiority and superiority. The thoughts and actions thus triggered can lead to aggression, inadequacy or even suicide. In moderation television can be illuminating, informative and reality investing, and in small amounts, as a quick-fix, it can help to relax and entertain. However, too much television threatens a realistic view of the world, distorts self-perception or blocks out real life altogether.

> A number of children said that they felt under pressure to look good because of their peers or the media. 'At school you are under pressure to be pretty, wear make-up and have the right figure. If not, you don't fit in. I don't like the way I look because I am not skinny or tall.' (13-year-old girl)

> A considerable number of comments focused on the fact that many girls feel they need to wear make-up. 'I can't go out without wearing nice clothes and make-up! Everyone says I'm too young but it makes me feel good about myself.' (Layard and Dunn, 2009, p. 4)

The seriousness of these trends hides a darker side: young people are being taught that behaving selfishly is acceptable. The imbalance is unsustainable at every level and has deep and enduring consequences. Society's unquestioning belief in consumerism conceals a deeper rejection of equality, as personal gain outweighs any notion of social justice. Reality-investing thoughts and actions (unlike giving in to quick-fix in the short term) achieve real goals and lasting wellbeing. In addition, acknowledging the positive impact on real life of specific thoughts and actions can substantially improve both physical and mental health:

> I found that teaching ten-year-old children the skills of optimistic thinking and action cuts their rate of depression in half when they go through puberty. (Seligman, 2002, p. 27)

There is a need to extend the aspects of the curriculum which may cover a wide range of themes, such as personal development of diet-related health routines; physical activity and sleep; learning about wellbeing and self-improvement; and social trends and economic development. None of this can be achieved without attention to developing collaborative, supportive teacher and practitioner relationships both within the school and between agencies.

Positive change may require that the adults in schools have the appropriate skills to invest in reality also. Teachers and practitioners influence real lives by understanding the theory, developing the practice and supporting the change. New realities are born not of old ideologies but new ideas. Inactivity on these issues is reality evading – therefore meaningful activity is not only necessary but key to everybody's success:

> We also signalled in *Aiming High for Young People* that enabling all young people to navigate successfully the increasingly complex and changing environment in which they grow up requires a new approach that focuses on building their resilience and affirms their place in society. . . . To support this, we are setting a goal that by 2020 all young people will be participating in positive activities to develop personal and social skills, to promote their wellbeing and to reduce the behaviour that puts young people at risk. (DCSF, 2007b, p. 128)

Physical activity

It is tempting to view television as an indomitable force that cannot be overthrown. Viewing time removes children from the physical and social activities that help form and deepen relationships, and underpin physical and mental health. Balance and range (as explored in Chapter 4) are key and, with these principles in mind, schools may be able to create more opportunities for physical activity with a view to increasing the positive factors influencing children's wellbeing.

While the physical fitness and resilience benefits of physical activity have been accepted for many years, the impact on mood is less well recognized. The 'feel-good factor' of physical activity so crucial to emotional wealth, is becoming more widely documented. According to the research the benefits are wide-ranging. They include:

- reduced anxiety
- improved mood
- better cognitive function

- less depression
- enhanced self-worth
- superior sleep quality.

Findings also suggest that benefits include the prevention and alleviation of a variety of mental health problems, although it is hard to identify direct links where positive impact is so broad. Research is still in its early stages but evidence does suggest that, with habitual and longer-lasting interventions, physical activity both reduces the onset and improves recovery from a number of diseases, and not solely for those at risk. Indeed, with its low cost implications and freedom from worrying side effects, physical activity appears to have purely positive impact. More importantly for schools, physical activity impacts on both learning and behaviour, so can help children to flourish in a way that few other interventions can claim (Biddle and Ekkekakis, cited in Huppert et al., 2005):

> Social support appears to be associated with physical activity in adults and youth . . . the 'motivational climate' created by such a leader may be vital in determining whether people return for future sessions . . . evidence suggests that the most positive climate will be when the exercise leader encourages cooperation and rewards effort over performance. (p. 156)

The role of physical activity in wellbeing should be more broadly defined than just sporting pursuits and competition. Physical activity can incorporate many hobbies that require mastery of physical movement. Examples include cooking, playing a musical instrument, gardening, dance and drama. In other words, physical activity includes any way of using the skeletal muscles that expends energy and raises heart and metabolic rates. To ensure fullest participation, physical activity needs to be balanced with cooperative rules, differentiated tasks and an element of **fun**. Therefore, schools that can offer children the widest possible *menu* of physical activities will help ensure every child stays active. More importantly, physical activity needs to be included across the curriculum if learners who do best on bodily-kinaesthetic intelligence are to get opportunities to do well. This more recent approach allows physical activity and recognizes it as equally important to academic learning. It also means that teachers and practitioners who develop physical activity will be valued as highly as their more 'academic' peers. The developmental model therefore alters to articulate physical activity as body-knowledge:

Increasing opportunities for sport at school and in the community

The trend towards reduced time spent on sport in the curriculum, as well as reduced sports facilities in schools, needs to be reversed. Girls are much less likely to take part in sports and therefore there needs to be a specific focus on creating appropriate sporting opportunities for them. (Shah and Marks, 2004, p. 7)

In a culture where reality-evading activity is widely acceptable, and watching television and eating junk food is perceived as desirable, consumption becomes a personal right. Unfortunately, this view further legitimizes the 'hedonic treadmill' – fuelling people's desire for more in spite of their inability to gain from their new circumstance – and fails to deliver on the pleasures the consumption is supposed to provide. This pushes use and often abuse to unhealthy extremes, causing more stress in addition to what is already an unhealthy lifestyle choice.

Social changes in leisure trends contribute to the negative factors added to young people's lives. Shopping, for example, is no longer considered a domestic routine but a conventional pastime. Living up to social comparison has become something of accepted addiction. Unfortunately the distortion caused by the media does little to diminish this tendency, and it is made worse by a human ability to adapt and habituate to new circumstance. In evolutionary theory, this habituation can be understood as useful, particularly when dealing with less recent challenges in human survival. The adjustment makes sense in the natural world: when things go badly it is a good insurance policy to keep wanting more, but when things go well the feeling dampens satisfaction – leading people to feel driven to *maximize* when *optimizing* is actually sufficient.

Take the preparation of food as an example, as relationships and food go hand in hand, mealtimes provided both structure and purpose for social interaction. Unfortunately communal meals are becoming rarer, and with them the loss of time that was made for preparing food and eating together – the skills people used to share – are vanishing. Again it is the poorest margins of the population that problems are most serious, when the cycle of deprivation inhibits the social habits that provide increased positive factors. When families cannot afford to have children's friends over for tea, there is no opportunity to share cooking skills or recipes or have the talks that give meaning to life:

Much of family routine is based around meals. A mother's love, courtship, and friendship are often expressed through giving food. (Huppert et al., 2005, p. 190)

Learning to cook is not a performance or a gift but a survival skill. As with so much social learning, the activity also involves the exchange of deeper messages. The conversations incidental to the activity are just as important:

[Schools need to] ensure that children and young people have opportunities to learn about different types of food in the context of a balanced diet (using 'the eatwell plate'), and how to plan, budget, prepare and cook meals, understanding the need to avoid the consumption of foods high in salt, sugar and fat and increase the consumption of fruit and vegetables. (Healthy Schools, 2009)

By focusing on nutrition and diet, there is a fear that schools will only have time to address the narrow aspect of food, without any of the social aspects that can make eating so beneficial. Watching someone else cook transfers more than ingredients and method, it is about caring, sharing and nurturing. Social occasions reinforce belonging and acceptance, the meaning of diversity and fair share, communication and exploration.

Keverne (Huppert et al., 2006) describes puberty as a period of brain development where young people become most vulnerable to behavioural problems such as eating disorders, addiction, depression and even suicide. These problems are not only occurring earlier but are also more prevalent among young women (for whom, as we have already seen, self-image and status are pivotal). Consumption and materialism have a knock-on effect on school life. In a culture driven by performance, celebrity status and the newest gadgets, wellbeing is often sidelined in favour of quicker routes to pleasure. The latest 'must-have' culture fuels an obsession in results, with a view to securing top jobs and buying a luxury lifestyle (James, 2007). School work becomes a route to personal positioning, not the discovery and life-long habit of learning to be enjoyed in its own right.

The social events linked to friends and home-life also create stress for young people at a time where body changes and high emotion can be overwhelming. During this stage, identity formation and self-esteem are central developmental issues. Evidence shows that having more than four close friends can help protect against depression:

One in 10 youngsters questioned in a survey disagreed that 'life was really worth living'. Those not in work or education were less likely to be happy. ... Chief executive Martina Milburn said: 'Young people tell us that family is key to their happiness, yet too often we find they don't have this crucial support. At the Prince's Trust we help vulnerable young people, steering them away from false support systems such as drugs, alcohol and dangerous gangs and providing them with a sense of purpose again.' (BBC Online News, 2009)

Some schools have taken the lead in the area of social learning, paying attention to lunch times, family learning sessions and grand-parent involvement in after-school clubs.

Mental health is developed as a preventative measure. Rather than tackle challenging behaviour through formal strategies and policy, they have invested in opportunities for physical activity and relationships to grow. In some schools pupils and students are actively engaged in creating relationship contracts, young people create their own 'ground rules' that they more readily accept, evaluate and regulate. As Andrew McColloch, Chief Executive Officer of the Mental Health Foundation explains, tackling emotional literacy is key to flourishing. He would like to see wider programme involving giving children skills in self-help techniques such as cognitive behavioural therapy:

> 'If you did that you would be increasing our emotional literacy overall. It's about building collective resilience,' he argues. Moreover, if people did become mentally unwell, they would find it easier to engage with psychological therapies. 'It's like having a physical accident – if you are physically fit, you are likely to rehabilitate faster.' (Pollock, 2009, p. 4)

Emotional literacy is developed through SEAL and other programmes that provide a basis for the exploration of actions and feelings.

Health and play

As the Good Childhood Report states, children see that their own behaviour influences their own experience of childhood and play is therefore vitally important. On the contrary, substance abuse and getting into trouble were the factors most often cited as contributing to poor childhood experience. In terms of health, alternative opportunities that also boost physical and mental capacity might have significant impact on young lives and school culture.

> If they think smoking or doing Drugs is a good part of there life it should be stopped. and they should think about what they are doing.
> ... Getting into trouble with police/family. Becoming addicted to substances.
> Hanging around the streets with the bad people cause there's not enough leisure places around. (Children's Society, 2009a, p. 6)

Brown (2005) explains the fundamental nature of play in a child's early social relationships: a baby's smile elicits a mother's cooing and babbling, which generate a rush of shared, bonding, emotions. In a sequence of playful interaction these actions deepen the bonding in a biological response: eye contact, mother smiles, baby smiles, right brain attunes. From these early communications evolve more complex interactions and the development of emotional control, for example the facilitation of responsive relationships through play.

The joyful feelings derived from play are intrinsically rewarding. However, we will see that, although pleasure in learning is important in its own right, play must not be confused with 'making learning activities fun'. Play provides opportunities for physical and emotional release. Risk, challenge and enthusiasm are good for health. Filer (2008) explains how sitting down in a classroom is a very recent feature of human learning activity and that movement is a much older means for children to make sense of their presence in the world. Running, jumping, skipping and other activity all lead to the development of physical strength, spatial awareness and movement control. Playful and physical activities are also important for mental health and the development of optimism. Seligman (1995) explains that when children develop control it increases enjoyment, meaning that they will try new actions and seek to expand this control, creating a positive feedback loop. Physical activity is not restricted to positive feelings and is an essential part of the development of physical understanding:

> Learning about self movement structures an individual's knowledge of the world – it is a way of *knowing*, and we actually, through movement and play, *think* in motion. For example the play-driven movement of leaping upward is a lesson about gravity as well as one's body. And it lights up the brain and fosters learning. Innovations, flexibility, adaptability, resilience, have their roots in movement. (National Institute for Play, 2006)

When children engage in pleasant activities, they also build their physical and mental strength and capacity. Cardiovascular activity raises longevity, and optimism fosters resilience and reduces susceptibility to a number of diseases. Later in life these attributes can help further real opportunities and achievements, underlining the benefits of experimentation and play.

Play provides a safe medium for children to explore the difference between positive *dreaming* and negative *fantasy*. Wishful daydreaming for self-motivation is very different from escapist fantasies that never relate to real-life scenarios: by understanding the distinction between the two, one can develop optimism and clearly attainable goals. Play allows children to experiment in both thought and action, thus enabling them later to opt for those with greatest reality-investing value in real life. Dreaming represents positive imagination, framing ideas in possibility and envisioning scenarios achievable in the future.

As Brown (2009) explains, rough-housing may look chaotic but it actually contributes to the development of social awareness, cooperation and fairness. When good-natured and between friends, the physical element of play should not be feared or controlled, but understood as important in emotional and physical development:

> A natural extension of the form – as it naturally diminishes with age – is lifelong involvement in games, sports and group activities that not only tolerate, but enjoy creative tension. Lack of experience with this pattern of play hampers the normal give and take necessary for social mastery, and has been linked to poor control of violent impulses in later life. (National Institute for Play, 2006)

Without opportunity for such play not only is physical strength at risk, but mental health is significantly inhibited and young people themselves behave in ways they themselves find difficult to cope with.

The significant contribution of play in terms of reality-investing activity depends on whether it helps achieve sustainable improvement in real life. Spending time on an Xbox® can be seen as a reality-evading activity, or in the short term a quick-fix activity giving momentary escapism, protecting a child from boredom or stress. However, isolating and inactive pastimes such as this could in the long term damage a child's social awareness and physical health. Balance is essential. Provided that passive forms of entertainment are viewed as short-lived pastimes they will probably not undermine long-term wellbeing.

Storytelling is another important part of play. It offers opportunities to develop the attitudes and beliefs that underpin individual decisions and choices. In a recent interview Robin Gibb (of the pop band, the Bee Gees) described vividly how he and his brothers used to sit by their radio telling stories about their plans for the future. While playing with tunes and writing songs, the scenarios they dreamed up were to become reality. Gibb identified the shared aspect of these early stories as important in forming their common vision – a desire to explore different sounds – which was central to their success. This anecdote clearly indicates the importance of telling stories and dreaming as sources of motivation, positive attitude and success. When supported by others the positive factors in shared vision increase the probability that the vision will be realized. Anything becomes possible when aim is shared. Expressing dreams aloud or on paper can enable the feelings and outcomes of innovation. Possibility flourishes further when children can trust in their close relationships and confide their most intimate hopes.

Pretend play extends the dreaming. The experience can feel very real and emotions apply to the moment – children are living their dream. Childhood play will turn into adult creativity and imagination only if it is encouraged and it can be diminished or extinguished if not supported or extended. Skilful adults will give the support and resources needed to broaden capacity and develop further through play:

The ability of the young child to create their own sense of their mind, and that of others, takes place through pretend play, which continues to nourish the spirit throughout life, and remains key to innovation and creativity. Deprivation studies uphold the importance of this pattern of play, as understanding and trusting others and developing coping skills depends on its presence. (National Institute for Play, 2006)

The nature of play equipment also needs careful consideration. Highly prescriptive games and branded toys may rob children of their own creativity, and simpler solutions that allow the mind to run free are generally preferable. In the following example, a diagnosis-led decision could have had worse consequences for a young boy with Down's syndrome. After being told by an educational psychologist that Down's children are unable to play, his parents gave away his toys. But, as an observer of the meeting noticed, the boy was running the TV remote control up and down the window ledge, using it very effectively as a toy car. The tale is a clear reminder that the labels and assumptions attached to some children can steal their most basic requirements:

Children are helped to extend their play if they have play props, but the play props need to be open to an imaginative response. Commercially made props have very limited value and they are expensive. They only encourage a narrow response from children. A plastic apple is usually played with as if it is an apple, a child can make whatever fruit or vegetable they want with a lump of dough! (Bruce, 2001, p. 86)

Clearly, play is a route to emotional flourishing and without it young people are restricted in choice and skill. As previously outlined, providing young people with opportunities to develop healthily, requires more than the skills and knowledge required for baseline survival. Being free from pain and safe from injury fall short of enabling creative, optimistic and successful internal lives, capable of engaging with reality.

Attitudes to play

Hawken (2007) identifies two distinct attitudes to play: *play-to-win* and *play-to-play*. Play-to-win (whether alone or with others) assumes a fixed target or goal which is typically attained at the expense of others. There can only be one winner, and when they are identified the game stops. Therefore the goal of a play-to-win game is the competition between players, and is nothing to do with the pleasure of the shared activity or the success in reaching a common goal. The competitive aspect of a play-to-win philosophy allows only for a narrow sense of achievement, i.e. doing better than someone else. It can never be a gauge of personal success or teamwork:

> Our entire economic system is predicated on competition. Our schooling trains us to beat others and regard them as obstacles to our own success. Even in our own families there is rivalry for attention and love and approval ... we can't even go dancing without getting involved in a dance contest. We need a working definition of competition:
>
> Competition is two or more people trying to achieve a goal that cannot be achieved by all of them. (Saidman, 1993)

Play-to-win therefore denies the sense of journey that is vital to human flourishing and which, irrespective of the target, takes all players to the boundaries of their capability. The target and performance culture (which we have already identified as damaging to children's wellbeing) clearly embodies a play-to-win philosophy.

On the other hand, play-to-play keeps players focused on the activity in hand and on the journey (or purpose) that makes the activity worthwhile:

> Cooperation means that the success of each participant is linked to that of each other and of every other. Studies show that in a co-operative environment, children encourage each other. They have improved communication and they trust each other more. They are more sensitive to each other's needs. (ibid.)

Playing-to-play articulates a more reality-investing philosophy, whether at the personal level of enjoying the activity and being involved, or at a group level (keeping others in the game). This philosophy also extends to communities (i.e. social justice) and to the environment (i.e. sustainability). Interestingly, in his interview, Robin Gibb expressed the band's desire to create a *different* type of music – an aim more akin to a play-to-play philosophy. He deplored the present state of the music business whose play-to-win desire for fame and fortune prefers to ape or outdo current top artists rather than exploring new sounds.

Enabling the game to continue is important, but fair play is particularly significant in keeping all players involved. Rules are vital to mark expectations and boundaries: without them, participants may become confused and anxious, and success is unclear and elusive (Diener and Biswas-Diener, 2008). Play rules can be seen as a parallel for adult policies: all participants need to understand their responsibility in upholding the rules for everyone's benefit – and to appreciate their right to change unfair rules:

Children and young people have told us the importance of respect, fairness and kindness. You should be bold in demonstrating these values in your relationships with others, both children and young people and adults. (What gives children and young people a good childhood? (Children's Society, 2009b, p. 11)

Encouraging children to play-to-play means developing flexible rules that include others and build cooperation, i.e. listening, helping each other and accommodating for different ability. The demonstration of equality (which often involves treating people differently) is inherent to fair play.

Without fair play, the feelings of failure and defeat imposed by an unfair culture of targets and performance indicators will result in people reaching for quick-fixes and reality-evading strategies. Unfortunately, these replace beneficial, reality-investing thoughts and actions. Then, children continue to lose confidence and capability. Where schools are committed to promoting self-esteem, educators will understand that there exists a vast difference between failure and defeat, although popular debate often confuses the two states. Every child has a chance to succeed as long as their success is not solely determined against the performance criteria of others. Playing-to-win focuses on the result or position, while playing-to-play draws attention to the effort, the speed and the distance. Children may feel *defeated* as a result of competing with others, but they can still celebrate their *success* if they achieve to the best of their ability. Competition and cooperation are not necessarily mutually exclusive when the philosophy is one of collaboration. In a play-to-play culture the rules allow the flexibility needed to accommodate different strengths and abilities. Working towards fair play among children – and thus between the adults they become – will create a culture that celebrates a level playing field of cooperation, trust and friendship.

Sustainability really comes to life in outdoor play. Interacting with an environment that is increasingly under threat gives play-to-play a whole new dimension. By providing the opportunity for children to develop an interest in the natural world, they take a step towards appreciating and conserving it. Nature offers a sense of connection with wider communities and ultimately with the planet: engaging the energy of young people may be a route to the planet's survival.

The philosophy underpinning the programme is based upon a desire to provide young children with an education which encourages a healthy active outdoor lifestyle alongside an appreciation of the wide natural world which will encourage them to have a natural awareness in later life. (Filer, 2008, p. 64)

Play is essential but the stakes are high. Any continued activity depends on scarce resources, so shared activity should be sensitive to these limitations. Respect for the environment may in fact be key to valuing the lives of others. Ultimately, individual survival may not only be dependent on collaboration, but an ability to reach harmony within the wider system by having consideration for the diversity this brings:

> ... making prudent use of natural resources and having some good old-fashioned outdoor fun, young children learn about the need to take an interest in the issues of healthy lifestyles, conservation and sustainable development in order to ensure a better quality of life for everyone now and for generations to come (Defra, 1999, cited in Filer, 2008, p. 64)

Children's spaces are currently under particular threat from economic imperatives, but depriving young people of natural habitats in which to play and learn could have serious implications for many generations. Children need both the time and range of places in which to play. Natural objects and materials could actually help develop young people's sense of social justice, while consumerist, commercial play props could be seen as part of the problem.

Health and social lives

According to Layard et al. (2009), depression is the cause of great misery. The World Health Organization states that mental illness and addiction cause nearly half of all impairments. Although it is important to understand the effects of deprivation and conflict, recent 'advances' in practice have not always increased the wider population's wellbeing. More worryingly (as we have identified), the present system causes stress that puts pressure on all participants.

Unresolved, inequality results in behaviour that reflects the frustration and anger felt and this may be seen as 'challenging' or 'hard to manage'. Evidence shows that both introverts and extroverts have more positive feelings when sharing activities with other people, so it is the *quality* (not the *quantity*) of peoples' relationships that matters. From the perspective of the schools, an emotionally healthy culture may be addressed in a number of ways. First, they may increase the opportunities for children to develop skills and knowledge about mental health so that they can better articulate their feelings. Second, they can provide teachers and practitioners with the essential training in emotional literacy, helping them to recognize and respond to mental difficulties before they advance into illness:

> Experts learnt that most children lead happy lives, but a minority were seriously troubled or disturbed. They think that mental health problems are one of the greatest barriers to a good childhood. (Children's Society, 2009b, p. 14)

As we have already outlined, twenty-first-century living imposes a great deal of stress, much of which is probably here to stay. Despite this, so much more can be done to equip young people to deal with it more effectively and thereby improve their lives. More needs to be done in terms of identifying the source of pressure – i.e. the egotistical behaviour of adults – that creates negative factors detrimental to children's health:

> Stress, worry and anxiety were regularly mentioned as things that prevented young people having a good life: *Less stress, less pressure, more well respected, social life.* (Children's Society, 2009b, p. 7)

Social pressure and lack of understanding play a large part in determining the way young people learn to cope with life. In the first instance, quick-fixes characterized by thoughts and actions that blur or distort perception provide immediate relief from emotional pains or frustration. The danger is that they may damage health in the medium or long term. This unconstructive engagement reflects a short-termism that increases pain and setbacks, and could indicate a tendency to indulge immediate wants irrespective (or even at the expense of) future needs.

7 Happiness and learning

Learning is ultimately a personal experience, and for maximum attention and engagement it must be positive. A positive approach to learning and an optimistic attitude towards personal growth does far more than make for enjoyment. Happiness unlocks creativity, enables flexibility of thought, allows openness to new information and makes learning meaningful.

A holistic approach to child development requires a more profound understanding of learning and intelligence. It demands the recognition of personal growth in which effort and progress in any subject and at any level is equally valuable. The understanding of intelligence as multiple, diverse, distinct and dynamic has barely been addressed in many contexts. Giving equal weight to all aspects of human intelligence, and giving children what they need individually and with flexibility to take control of their own portfolio of strengths, is still an idea too difficult for many to envisage in practice. To prioritize the pleasure of learning necessitates wider choice, allowing the learner to take both control and responsibility. This requires a fundamental change in the teacher–learner relationship: only learners have the depth of personal knowledge – their strengths, weaknesses, likes and dislikes – ensuring their own pleasure in the learning activity.

Engagement demands that we put children's choice first, for no system can determine what young people like and enjoy. Greater flexibility in meeting the needs of young people will also mean that schools will promote the success of an increasing number of different children. However, flexibility requires a different understanding of intelligence – and most importantly what intelligence is *for*.

> If we fail to promote a full sense of people's abilities through education and training, as we have done for some generations, some – perhaps most – will never really discover what their real intellectual capacities are. In a crucial sense they never really know who they are or what they might become. (Robinson, 2001, p.109)

By highlighting for learners the elements that underpin their happiness, their self-understanding and their motivation for success, we can enable them both to take greater responsibility for learning and to flourish.

Defining happiness

In the context of education, we need to define happiness more clearly than the common and vague notions of heightened pleasure or absence of pain. There is a widespread assumption that happiness is somewhat frivolous and trivial, a secondary by-product removed from 'true' educational purpose. While most teachers and practitioners would see it as an important factor, some still say that it has little to do with learning and is therefore not worthy of priority in schools. However, happiness should be understood in terms of its specific implications for learning and its long-term impact on wellbeing.

Research shows that 'subjective wellbeing' measures correlate closely to feelings of happiness, so schools can determine levels of wellbeing with accuracy by asking children how happy they are. In view of recent changes this is essential information: from now on, schools need to take happiness seriously in order to evaluate the effectiveness of their methods, policies and strategies on learners' wellbeing.

Our arguments in the following sections are founded on the three dimensions of happiness which, according to Seligman (2007), make up a 'full life'. They differ in terms of application: some can be learned more than others and, therefore, if addressed in schools will produce more changes for wellbeing. However, they are all worthy of consideration because together they provide what is essential to enabling learners to flourish. Furthermore, the skills and knowledge that influence them differ from those that reduce the pain and suffering discussed in Chapter 5. This explains why vulnerable children are particularly left wanting.

There is a further long-term dimension: present happiness is critical to future happiness: the unhappy individual cannot imagine a positive future:

> We cannot feel good about an imaginary future when we are busy feeling bad
> about an actual present. (Gilbert, 2006, p. 124)

So from a pedagogical perspective, happiness is perceived as relatively fixed and genetically influenced, but research has not yet been able to determine how far it can be increased with new understanding, skills and knowledge. It remains to be seen how fresh insight into the plastic and trainable nature of intelligence can help schools to more effectively enhance learner happiness. On balance, evidence supports the idea that, through enjoyable activity, active engagement and an active understanding of happiness, more can be done to ensure that all children can flourish.

Broaden-and-build theory

According to Seligman (2007), three routes to happiness enable a 'full life': these are the 'pleasant', the 'good' and the 'meaningful' life. Together they enable young people to flourish, as they prevent what he terms an 'empty life'. These dimensions have been used to underpin the following sections. It is worth noting that they all differ, and some can be changed more easily than others through practice and training. However, a person who can engage through all three dimensions will have a 'fuller life' than a person who engages with one or two. Essentially, the life satisfaction produced by addressing the three lives combined appears to be greater than the sum of the parts, and is therefore the most successful route to flourishing.

Frederickson's broaden-and-build theory (in Huppert et al., 2005) adds strength to Seligman's ideas of what makes a 'pleasant life'. In the next two sections we outline the impact that positive feelings have on strength and resilience in learning. The fact that positive feelings make stronger learners in the short term, but more importantly develop long-term resilience, clearly underlines why learners' present happiness is so vital to their continued wellbeing. In a system permitted to restrict opportunity, a denial of the central nature of such feelings neglects present needs and will have far-reaching consequences in later years:

> I argue that positive emotions also produce optimal functioning, not just within the present, pleasant moment, but over the long-tern as well. The bottom line message is that people should cultivate positive emotions in themselves and in those around them, not just as end states in themselves, but also as a means to achieving psychological growth and improved psychological and physical well-being over time. (Frederickson cited in Huppert et al., 2005, p. 217)

As we saw in Chapter 5, negative attitudes not only add to the achievement-capping stress, but also prevent a whole range of feelings that enhance the learning experience. Negative feelings reduce children's field of attention and focus them on the current experience or perceived threats. In contrast, positive feelings expand the range of children's thoughts and actions. When happy, they accumulate skills because they act in more alert and inquisitive ways. Enjoyable experiences therefore support flexible, creative and clearer thinking (Frederickson, cited in Huppert et al., 2005).

It is important to view young people's pleasure in learning activities as more than a way of 'having fun'. It is in fact fundamental to the development of skills for optimal learning. Being happy is not just pleasant. It has a greater function – a positive effect on cognition. When children find an activity pleasurable they remain engaged in learning and therefore gain more from their extended time on task.

Enjoying learning is hardly new. However, the idea persists that fun is for break-time or, more worryingly, for the time when young people leave school. 'Work hard now, get good grades, **then** you'll be able to have fun.' Statements such as these are profoundly misguided. It is crucial that children have the positive feelings that give them the physical, intellectual and social resources they need to enrich their present experience.

Various positive feelings have different effects which combine to enhance the learning experience. For example, joy increases motivation, creativity and the urge to play; interest increases exploration and the ability to take in new information; and contentment allows us to sit back and savour, allowing integration and consolidation (Frederickson, cited in Huppert et al., 2005). Csikszentmihályi (1996) describes these last feelings as important in the balance needed for creativity. A primitive urge that gives people pleasure when they are comfortable and relaxed enables recuperation time. Without this, the heightened activity associated with exploration leaves them unable to cope with future and unexpected events. Because learners cannot anticipate what the future holds, feeling good about something new needs to have its own rewards, so finding enjoyment in new activities can explain why creativity is so rewarding. The issue of balance is a core theme and worthy of note: too much or too little of a particular thing may be negative and damaging.

Skills and interest

Human beings are complex, intricate organisms which start life with roughly the same amount of 'building material'. Differences emerge as skills are developed in different ways. The direction of individual development depends very much on what children enjoy. Pleasure is derived from the ability to do certain activities and the skill to do them well. Every child is unique. None will share the same experience, so their feelings toward different activities will affect their choice and impact differentially on skill development.

Although intelligence is malleable and capable of growth, brain capacity is finite and children's development requires flexible handling to respect this plasticity. Intelligence needs to be recognized as highly diverse, and the ability to develop a wide variety of skills as critical to enabling every child's achievement As we previously identified with respect to optimum levels, the trade-off linked to specialization is far from straightforward. Different skills can be acquired through different approaches benefiting all types of intelligence at appropriate levels. Inequality develops when children are expected to fit a narrow and formalized progression. This unfairness is reinforced by testing methods developed to assess linguistic and logical skills to academic targets, and is unjust on those whose skills and abilities are not recognized by schools. The school system has traditionally valued certain areas of specialization above others, deepening learner inequity. In the short term this impairs development for all, as a whole range of skills are marginalized by the curriculum even though they may be equally important to economic activity in the long term:

> An exclusive focus on linguistic and logical skills in formal schooling can short change individuals with skills in other intelligences. It is evident from inspection of adult roles ... that spatial, interpersonal, or bodily-kinaesthetic skills play key roles. Yet linguistic and logical skills form the core of most tests of 'intelligence' and are placed on a pedagogical pedestal in our schools. (Gardner, 1993, p. 31)

Ultimately, this demands a personalized and differentiated curriculum that improves learner understanding. Children need to learn about multiple intelligences so that they can appraise their own strengths and weaknesses: this is vital to their future success.

Few schools are free from the pressures that result from organizational structures. Therefore, the unspoken expectation is that individuals will conform to a linguistic and logical process. Thus, the real power lies in the *administration* of teaching rather than in the development of learning and skills. Such deference to the system explains the difficulties many teachers and practitioners experience when trying to conceptualize the personalizing learning agenda. In effect, old ideology overpowers new knowledge.

> The conflation of academic ability with intelligence is simply taken for granted. It is in this sense an ideology. Like many ideologies, this one persists despite all evidence of the contrary. (Robinson, 2001, pp. 80–1)

It is easier to value all development when we recognise that every child needs an equal amount of resources and a finite number of options in which to excel. Furthermore, this highlights the unfairness of a system which values only certain aspects of growth in a limited number of skills.

Diversity of perception is such that children will experience classroom activity differently depending on their sensitivities, experience and background. Children start school having learned a great deal through interaction, experimentation and exploration – for learning is continuous. Therefore it is essential to understand young learners' background and context in order to enhance their development:

> . . . our view of the world is not only affected by what we can perceive; it is deeply influenced by other factors, which affect what we actually do perceive: the ideas, the values and beliefs through which we frame our understanding of it. (Robinson, 2001, p. 118)

This concept of personal experience is clearly demonstrated in the following example. A school in Bradford identified that young people that were not retaining knowledge from history lessons despite being engaged with and using the content. The majority of students were from a Pakistani background. They had very little personal context in which to place the history curriculum. The lesson failed to build on experience, a fact that was critical to finding a solution. Teachers found new local history perspectives and used examples that built more closely on students' lives. They used stories about the labour shortages which prompted mill owners to import labour after World War II, and they explained how Pakistani men were now seen as adding to local economic prosperity. By using young people's own ideas and understanding, they were able to place themselves more positively in a wider historical context. Most importantly, from a broaden-and-build perspective, it was by understanding the learners' background that enabled teachers to design relevant, meaningful lessons. Learning increased dramatically as young people shared their experience and stories with other family members. This helped to consolidate their understanding and pass it on to others.

This example demonstrates that when interests and backgrounds are properly understood and acknowledged, teachers and practitioners can respond to learner individuality with flexibility:

> They should listen to children and young people more and use their ideas. They just listen to adults and ignore children. Young person – Online survey (DCFS, 2008, p. 74)

Choice and option

Forces in education conspire to diminish options. Unfortunately, the impact is most severe on those whose skills and preferences fall outside more traditional subjects and methodologies. More significantly, from a happiness perspective, lack of opportunity curtails choice to options that may not be enjoyable. Furthermore, it denies the learners' responsibility: since they lack insight into the strengths and weaknesses of their own intelligence, they cannot make informed choices. Intelligence needs to be understood in greater depth by learners themselves so they can make better decisions which suit their learning, and make better choices even where options are limited:

> The paucity of our understanding of learning is often reflected in the lack of any shared or common agreement between teachers, let alone learners, as to what the process actually involves. . . . [Learning] is usually judged as a product rather than a process – 'I have learned this'. (West-Burnham and Coates, 2005, p. 34)

The development of a 'shared and common agreement' of what constitutes learning is rarely addressed in practice. As a consequence, decisions can be made without any thought as to who holds control. Teachers and practitioners can subconsciously organize teaching in ways that suit their delivery: unfortunately this does not always suit the learners' strengths.

All the evidence suggests that high attainment at school, college and university does not necessarily make people any happier in the long term. Income only makes people happier if they find ways of enjoying life *irrespective* of income; the deciding factor is that they feel in control and can therefore exercise choice (Nettle, 2005). Although the level of education does facilitate occupational choice, it seems that autonomy is a more profound determinant of wellbeing. It indicates a sense of empowerment in the situations that life brings. It is important for children to identify the activities they find enjoyable early on, so that they can spend the time required for expertise to develop and reach the confidence that brings such control. If they are not able to do this, either because their range of opportunities is too limited or because unenlightened teaching puts them off learning altogether, many will end up feeling stupid and powerless:

> One problem with our current society is that we have an attitude towards education as if it is there to simply make you more clever, make you more ingenious . . . the most important use of knowledge and education . . . is to effect changes from within to develop a good heart. (Dalai Lama and Cutler, 1998, p. 36)

The oppressive effect created by a testing culture can provoke both the aggressive or passive behaviour that characterizes disengagement. In the following example, Brooks describes the positive effect on a child's achievement when she is released from an environment that stifles her pleasure:

> It is notable that Rosie preferred to complete at home the tropical island book she designed at school. Her father says that she now prefers to write here, where she colours in her library carefully. Writing at school has become boring to her, he suspects because the teaching has lately been focused towards SATS outcomes. (Brooks, 2006, p. 43)

Happiness in learning will be further increased by facilitating a learner's decisions over his or her chosen direction (i.e. increasing learner control) and by adding elements of personal choice. Sadly, while education still operates on fixed outcomes, learner control is diminished through its very organization: the learner is *controlled* by having to fit the system. This has a negative impact on happiness as control is essential to wellbeing; lack of control has negative consequences:

> Being effective – changing things, influencing things, making things happen – is one of the fundamental needs with which human brains are naturally endowed ... gaining control can have a positive impact one's health and well-being, but losing control can be worse than never having had it at all. (Gilbert, 2006, pp. 20–2)

'To reflect the importance of choice, learners require more control and clearer alternatives that incorporate multidisciplinary approaches. This approach would involve recognizing that intelligence and its development comprise a physical relationship with the world and an emotional response to them, and not simply the ability to *think* about them. Learning certainly depends on thought but it rests also on movement, feeling and the vast breadth of human experience.

Resilience

Continuing this dimension of happiness which Seligman calls the 'pleasant life', we add the long-term dimension with the purpose of identifying and enhancing the present skills that have lasting effects on wellbeing. As we have seen, happiness facilitates physical and psychological strength, and these are pivotal in building young people's resilience. Finding positive meaning in daily experience, despite its trials and tribulations, is key to feeling satisfied with life. The positive relationship between feeling and meaning is not only reciprocal but also cumulative:

> Put differently, to the extent that the broaden-and-build effects of positive emotions accumulate and compound over time, positive emotions carry the capacity to transform individuals for the better, making them healthier and more

socially integrated, knowledgeable, effective and resilient. In short, the theory suggests that positive emotions fuel human flourishing. (Frederickson, cited in Huppert et al., 2005, p. 231)

Finding positive meaning after the most difficult experiences creates positive feelings. In turn, these increase the likelihood of a positive attitude towards future events. Children's resilience increases with their ability to consider wider perspectives and diverse solutions in the face of life's problems. It is supported by the mind's ability to produce positive feelings in response to bad experiences. Contrary to popular belief, most people report little change in their usual levels of happiness three months after a bad experience, and with hindsight even the worst events are often perceived as positively life enhancing (Gilbert, 2006).

Day-to-day emotions are harder to influence. However, evidence suggests that habits learned in a few months can increase positive feelings years later on: these include appreciation of present situation and deriving positive meaning from recent events. Such elements are easily built into the school day. For example, teachers may start the day with an appreciation of the things children enjoy and conclude with acknowledgement of what has been learned. Simple routines can set habits that years later could prevent depression and enhance positive feelings overall (Frederickson, cited in Huppert et al., 2005; Gilbert, 2006).

In a complex and demanding world, children can only be partly protected from problems: by its very nature, learning involves risk, disappointment and failure. Gladwell (2008) explains the value of a positive attitude to staying on-task in order to develop new understanding when faced with complex problems. He asserts that on average people need 10 years (or 10,000 hours) to become an expert, 'the brain takes this long to assimilate all that it needs to know to achieve true mastery'. Robinson et al. (2005) further highlight the importance of mistakes as an intrinsic part of successful learning and creativity. He redefines 'failure' in the words of Sir Harold Kroto, the Nobel Prize-winning scientist, as 'incremental steps toward a breakthrough'.

The broaden-and-build theory suggests that if this continues, most learners will be shaped by an ideology that, in contrast, divides and diminishes. Some children will be stifled, but more worryingly it will marginalize those whose abilities are hardest to identify. Education needs to pay much closer attention to understanding each child's multiple, distinctive and dynamic intelligence needs. Teachers can create opportunities for learners to enjoy what they do in less linguistic or analytical media than pen and paper, for instance using art, drama or cookery. This should enable children to find activities in which they want to develop expertise from an earlier age.

Barriers, boundaries and balance

The second of Seligman's dimensions of happiness is the 'good life'. It differs from the pleasant life in that it is more malleable and responds well to training: it relies less on pleasure which has a fixed quality and is susceptible to habituation. Schools can therefore have greater direct impact on happiness *per se* by applying these ideas in practice.

The pleasant life is said to be 25–50 per cent inherited (Seligman, 2005), However it is too simplistic to say that pleasant feelings are predetermined. Research cannot as yet measure the benefits of teaching children the techniques that impact on brain wiring, but such techniques could have long-term implications for wellbeing. People have a 'happiness set-point', a disposition that is more or less cheerful (Layard, 2005; Gilbert, 2006). This can be affected by changes in attitude and belief but such modifications demand long-term intervention. In addition, people's enjoyment fades over time, so the feelings of reward children derive from interesting and new activity will dissipate unless different ways of doing it are found or the level of difficulty increases. Therefore, addressing happiness means doing more than providing enjoyment. The choice of activity is important, but the level of engagement must also be right. Csikszentmihályi's (1996) flow theory helps to explain the role played by risk and its contribution to children's happiness. Flow can be observed when children are deeply engrossed in play, for example:

> ... it often involved painful, risky, difficult activities that stretched the person's capacity and involved an element of novelty and discovery. This optimal experience is what I called *flow*, because many of the respondents described the feeling when things were going well as an almost automatic, effortless, yet highly focused state of consciousness.(Csikszentmihályi, 1996, p. 110)

In order to provide the complexity that adds novelty, there needs to be an element of risk without harmful pain. Through risk, children find out where their boundaries lie. Boundaries are important because they provide safe limits for innovation, exploration and creativity. Beyond the boundaries, children lose their sense of safety and experience stress. For example, a familiar classroom where children feel comfortable provides a boundary within which confidence grows and discovery can take place. In contrast, an unfamiliar teacher adds a barrier to learning. In addition, if the new teacher's explanation is too complicated, children will become confused, pressurized and unable to participate:

... the distinction between 'risk' and 'hazard' is not sufficiently understood when considering children's activities. 'Risk is to inherent the human endeavour,' they write, 'and for children not to engage with it is for them to be cut off from an important part of human life in the interest of 'child protection'. People learn to assess and manage risk by encountering it. (Brooks, 2006, p. 34)

While it is important for children to make use of opportunities for risk and to experience as few barriers to learning as possible, they also need to function within safe boundaries. Here, choice once again plays a role: getting the balance right is vital and only the child is capable of gauging how he or she feels given any situation. A child's ability to weigh up his or her own progress, first through teacher guidance and later on through self-feedback, demands both good relationships and a flexibility of options. Without these there will be little opportunity to master the control and enable responsibility. Developing accountability and awareness of personal capability is fundamental: without risk, some activities actually become hazardous.

Children themselves need to understand the difference between boundaries and barriers, to negotiate the balance so critical to their happiness and vital to their learning. Stress can occur at any extreme, and prolonged imbalance has serious consequences for wellbeing. Degrees of comfort are important, as accelerating the pace is as oppressive as hindering engagement in the first place. By starting from the child's point of interest and building in different levels of choice and option, teachers and practitioners provide an ongoing incentive that motivates broad and varied skill development. In turn this ensures that children can regularly identify and reassess their goals:

> [People] naturally set themselves goals that involve some challenge, and happiness depends on having goals that are sufficiently stretching but can also be accomplished. Goals give meaning to life. However, a sensible person chooses goals whose pursuit he enjoys. There is not much sense in trying to accomplish things that give no joy ... Those who do end up depressed. (Layard, 2005, p. 114)

A belief in a fixed, linear intelligence rather than a multiple, growing capacity can help to alienate children from school altogether. In addition, certain stereotypes can lead to assumptions about risk that can be just as detrimental as the barriers created through prejudiced expectation.

Although attainment levels at school (such as high exam grades) are good indicators of life chances, they are poor indicators of success. Other factors such as the level of engagement obtained from work and leisure activities have a greater effect on long-term happiness than to corporate status or income. In other words, an individual's choice to become a lawyer (when his or her hobby is gardening) or a landscape designer (who has a passion for crime fiction) will have a more significant impact on life chances than the attainment of grade C+ in Maths, English and Biology.

Furthermore, evidence shows that educational qualifications can heighten an individual's perception of inequality, particularly in fields and organizations where competition is high. In the final analysis, the deciding factor is the engagement people find in their work activity, so qualifications only increase happiness for those who can make the *right* choices and suit their strengths more easily (Diener and Biswas-Diener, 2008).

Engagement is a very personal affair. The capacity to be happy on one's own is a skill which, coupled with autonomy (as discussed previously), adds to personal satisfaction:

> In his book *Solitude*, Anthony Storr makes a compelling case for intimate personal relationships . . . 'Yet if it is desirable to foster the growth of the child's imaginative capacity,' he wrote, 'we should ensure that our children, when they are old enough to enjoy it, are given time and opportunity for solitude.' Solitude not only fosters creativity, argued Storr, but relates to an individual's capacity to connect with and manifest their own true inner feelings. (Brooks, 2006, p. 45)

Positive attitude and deeper belief

It is the aspect of finding deeper meaning and having a purpose in life that underpins the next section. From a philosophical standpoint it is the right place to ask: is life about making money? Or is there a more profound purpose to being alive? Ideas from philosophy, religion and, more recently, positive psychology all seem to agree that without clear purpose people drift and become unhappy. People are happier when having identified their strengths; they put them to good and meaningful use:

> People who achieve a sense of meaning in their lives *are* happier than those who live from one pleasure to another. Carol Ryff of the University of Wisconsin has provided ample evidence of this. She has compiled refined measures of such things as purpose in life, autonomy, positive relationships, personal growth and self-acceptance and used them to construct an index of psychological well-being. (Layard, 2005, p. 22)

Can schools ensure that young people develop these skills, as well as understanding why they are relevant to their lives? We know that nature can be greatly influenced by nurture: happiness levels can be increased with intentional effort and deliberate action. If these skills are so important to young people's lives, why are they not seen as higher priorities?

> ... we also expect that with a few years, practice and coaching will begin to have their remedial effects, innocence will yield to experience and education, and pooing errors will disappear altogether. So why doesn't this analysis extend to errors of every kind? ... if practice and coaching can teach us to keep our pants dry, then why can't they teach us to predict our emotional futures? (Gilbert, 2006, p. 196)

It seems reasonable to assume that, given its importance and impact on our lives, happiness should be accorded a higher priority in education. If an optimistic outlook can so profoundly impact on young people's learning and prevent certain mental difficulties, then it is crucial to address the issue more carefully in practice. So the only way to teach young people about happiness is to ensure that they *are* happy at any given time, and not as a reward for a present activity which itself might be unrewarding. Similarly, happiness needs to be measured as a present *quantity*: it is useless as a retrospective or anticipatory measure. Once this is properly understood by all, happiness becomes a more tangible outcome and teaching will be acknowledged as a priority.

Putting personal happiness first is fundamental to making learner choice possible, as it places emphasis on learner control. This in turn enables all children (irrespective of ability) to choose to do what they enjoy. It also means young people can more easily build on what they already know, or may develop in areas they feel weakest. By understanding their personal strengths and weaknesses, they will also grow in strength and resilience.

In terms of education purpose and from a rights perspective, making sure young people are happy could be the new priority that enables a more value-based pedagogy. Ensuring that all children have an opportunity to develop the skills and understanding they need, to this end also delivers on fairness and equity. By focusing on the changes needed for this to happen, we also challenge the current harmful classifications. Strategies developed to facilitate enjoyment, engagement and full participation go far beyond acceptance – they demonstrate tolerance and compassion. There can never be a scale on which to categorize children from the most to the least happy, so this also removes the tendency of having to divide them into arbitrary groups according to merit. As routes to happiness are made from very different combinations of all three lives outlined above, no particular combination can be seen as more worthwhile. Not only do different combinations offer a unique way to personal growth, but the overall gain from all three is larger than the benefits of engaging in simply one or two. This synergy gives us an added dimension which relates to the strength of diversity. For teachers and practitioners, accepting that all children have a need to reach the 'fullest life' possible is fairer than defining their merit by testing, and articulates more equitably what is understood by potential. As Ainscow explains, a definition of 'social exclusion' or 'inclusion' based on academic or social criterion is misleading, for it implies the existence of forms of exclusion that are *not* social and are therefore acceptable (Ainscow and Dyson, 2006).

8 Inclusive practice and valuing learning

In the last chapter we established that, in order to promote wellbeing, the learning experience must be enjoyable. This chapter looks at how changes in a school's culture and approach to learning can support a richer, more enjoyable learning experience. Because, as opportunities and strategies for change are developed, learner happiness is taken seriously, while failing to fully engage with this priority effectively neglects learner wellbeing.

In the following sections we outline two theories relating to these issues in the context of teaching practice. The first idea is the 'growth mindset' which we will explore in relation to language and measuring effort. Dweck's 'psychology of success' explains how the celebration of effort enhances learner engagement and thus enables a shared approach to the broaden-and-build theory outlined earlier. The second idea – developing belonging – explores ways to increase learner self-esteem, by enhancing the child's sense of belonging within the school community. In essence, cultures that truly value learning, celebrate effort and develop learner ownership are more likely to promote the greatest learner wellbeing.

Developing a 'learning culture' often requires a substantial shift in a shared understanding of what constitutes learning. The problems in letting go of what the dominant teaching culture is, must not be underestimated. A school's expression of the value it places on learning is a strong indicator of its ability both to teach responsively and achieve successful culture change. Tackling culture is never easy.

Cultures might be best understood as ecosystems created by the interaction of living organisms; each species within the system depends on the mutualism of those relationships to insure long-term survival:

> The blessing of the existence of many languages is that they interact, change and grow ... there is no stable ecosystem or language, but only systems growing and changing in a dynamic process of evolution ... almost all indigenous people

recorded life as a linguistic continuum, because their survival depended on such an intimate relationship to land and one another. Their bodies were not something that merely carried their brain around, but an entire sensate organ wedded to their habitat and tribe. (Hawken, 2007, pp. 99–100)

In the same way, school culture evolves as practice develops; the two are linked together in an evolving relationship. As teachers' and practitioners' language changes to articulate learning as holistic and more than brain activity alone, their practice will in turn change to reflect this. Patterns in nature mirror those in culture. The waves made by changing norms are long and shallow, and difference emerges only slowly because every participant lives the culture differently. By contrast, process, strategy and language can be rapidly altered; the wavelengths are shorter, speeding shifts in practice. However, the two are closely linked, so schools will only achieve a culture shift if they are able to develop and embed new ideas and allow time. To do so schools urgently need to identify the ideas and language that will make a positive difference to culture. We return to the importance of developing a nurturing environment when we explore 'belonging' in the final section of this chapter.

Fullan's findings on reflective action (2007) also support the assertion that behaviours and emotions change before beliefs. A learning cycle that strengthens understanding can alter the process by attaching new meaning to action. In other words, if we teach differently we obtain different results. Only then do attitudes change. Underlying teaching is an idea that schools are there to fill gaps in learners' knowledge. Wellbeing, however, cannot be understood from this perspective which is at best counterproductive and at worst damaging. A wellbeing approach builds on capacity. McKnight's insights are expressed by Block:

> In the professional world of service providers, whole industries have been built on people's deficiencies … John sees a system as an organized group of funded and well-resourced professionals who operate in the domain of cases, clients and services. As soon as you professionalize care, you have produced an oxymoron. He says that systems are capable of service, not care. (Block, 2008, pp. 13–14)

Gladwell (2008) describes the effect that selection has on hockey players. An analysis of birthdates shows that physical development affects the chances of young players' entry to top leagues. Older players are selected in preference to younger ones, giving them greater opportunities for practice, proficiency and therefore progress in the game. Unfortunately, the trade-off is that many talented young people whose birthdays fall later in the year miss out simply because of physical immaturity. In the same way, basic numeracy and literacy are 'learning to learn' skills that are fundamental to effective learning, and children who fail to master them early on are consequently more likely to give up trying to learn them. Thus, poor basic skills cumulatively slow down engagement in more complex learning. The gap widens further as success, reward and enjoyment wane.

Recent changes in the Early Years Foundation Stage propose a different approach. The guidance expresses growth and development as an uneven and complex process. With age and stage no longer expressed as synonymous, different progression routes become feasible and can be appreciated and recognized as successful. Learning is therefore understood to differ greatly from more linear interpretations of development that emphasize academic progression based on a concept of fixed ability.

Children who fall behind will disengage at a much higher rate than others because participation in school becomes harder and enjoyment is diminished. If young people are unhappy in the classroom they will be unable to grow and improve their learning skills. As others become stronger, more proficient learners, those who struggle become progressively weaker and less resilient. This would also explain why the move to secondary school has such influence on children, even allowing for the impact of transition:

> Secondary school children seem to become bored, stop learning and no longer enjoy the activities available at school. All of these problems are certain to undermine children's curiosity and personal development, as getting involved in activities that they find interesting and challenging, and learning from such experiences, are all key factors in developing children's potential. (Shah and Marks, 2004, p. 27)

It is the duplicity of systemic prejudice that enables some children to appear to fill the stereotypes 'gifted and talented'. However, the cost across the board is huge in terms of talent, as children who are more advanced are given greater encouragement and more opportunities, leaving their peers at a significant disadvantage on both counts. Within a system that consistently treats some children as 'gifted', there is injustice which impacts on everyone including the 'high achievers'. In the long term these children will only fulfil their potential if their effort is not affected: if they stop perceiving effort as the key to achievement, they too will cease to practice and are just as likely to fail as more modest learners. With regard to wellbeing, this is fundamental: as research from Duke University, North Carolina, shows anxiety and depression among undergraduates who aspire to 'effortless perfection' – high grades without having to try (Dweck, 2007).

Where learning is valued, accesses to the opportunities to learn are an overarching priority. Insisting on wider access to curriculum content also lessens the focus on targets, as Bunch explains from a Canadian perspective:

> Where inclusion has succeeded in Canada the curriculum is regarded as a tool, not as a controlling agent. It is viewed as flexible. It is to be attuned to an individual pace of learning. Students in the same classroom can learn together, though they may be at differing parts of the curriculum. In other words, curricula are designed for universal access for all learners, when inclusion is the objective. (Bunch, 2005, p. 3)

Valuing learning, places more importance on progress and effort and diminishes the negative impact of attainment. A positive change in practice would be to publish improvement scores rather than test results, taking emphasis away from final position and re-focusing on improvement. As Dweck describes:

> People with the growth mindset, however, believe something very different. For them, even geniuses have to work for their achievements ... They may appreciate endowment, but they admire effort, for no matter what your ability is, effort is what ignites that ability and turns it into accomplishment. (Dweck, 2006, p. 41)

From a wellbeing perspective, a belief in growth (as opposed to fixed ability) is fundamental to the development of resilience and engagement in learning. An appreciation of growth through effort must therefore be clearly articulated in both practice and language.

Definitions of 'inclusion' vary because the term has a legacy of different meanings according to context. In education the whole notion of inclusion is still widely debated within a system that retains grammar, comprehensive and 'special' schools, and many existing definitions are highly contradictory. From a growth perspective it may be most useful to use the following, put forward by Ainscow and Dyson (2006):

> Inclusion is concerned with all children and young people in schools; it is focused on presence, participation and achievement; inclusion and exclusion are linked together such that inclusion involves the active combating of exclusion; and inclusion is seen as a never-ending process. Thus an inclusive school is one that is on the move, rather than one that has reached a perfect state. (Ainscow and Dyson, 2006, p. 25)

In this text, 'inclusive practice' has been deliberately chosen to reflect the understanding that developing inclusive cultures takes a great deal of time and effort. Furthermore, it reinforces the idea that practice and ideas are subject to change through revaluation and development. The emphasis is on practice, which means to do something repeatedly in order to adapt and improve: it implies preparation, rehearsal and improvement. To approach inclusive practice correctly, all educators will need to speak a shared language that reflects this growth dimension. Learning is ongoing and its value needs to be clearly articulated using a language that reflects an understanding of growth. Referring to inclusion (as distinct from inclusive practice) suggests a fixed, attainable target rather than a dynamic, developing culture. Inclusive practice is an organic process: rather than offering a fixed alternative to the existing culture, it builds on current perspectives with personalized practice. These ideas add to the personal dimension of the 'broaden-and-build' theory in the last chapter by developing a shared understanding and new strategies and by transforming culture.

However, although inclusive practice must not be seen as 'mainstreaming' the difficult or the needy, it makes little sense if it occurs at the expense of vulnerable children's needs. True inclusive practice can only be achieved by addressing inequality for all. Without this, the threat to wellbeing continues. Crucially, education needs to move towards a personalized service: a caring and nurturing culture that respects learner individuality and diversity. Where targets and performance preside, schools will continue to discriminate: quite simply, there's not room enough at the top for everyone. There is, however, always room for growth: improvement and effort can always be assessed equally:

> Inclusion: personalisation applies equally to the gifted and talented and those with special needs. In many ways it offers a powerful strategy to ensure optimum provision for all young people that is geared to their particular needs and talents. (National College for School Leadership, 2009, p. 8)

Bunch describes how Canada has shifted from a teaching service to learner-centred organizations with an approach rooted in rights and values:

> Where inclusive education in Canada is successful, all learners are viewed as true learners, true learners at their own levels of ability. Learning more powerfully than most, as with students labelled gifted or talented is still learning. Learning more modestly than most, also, is still learning. (Bunch, 2005, p 6)

Also, evidence from the UK shows that, irrespective of their differences, all learners can be successfully included in appropriately accommodated mainstream schools (Mason and Dearden, 2004). However, the challenge is to turn atypical practice into a cultural norm. Ultimately, inclusive practice will vary for every classroom, department or school, and delivery should always be unique to every individual child.

Once inclusive practice is seen from a growth perspective, it is easier to understand the impact on culture: growth suggests improvement and simply acknowledging this possibility raises aspirations. In addition, motivation allows hope, and the understanding that small-scale strategies affect wider change, and without small changes a wider culture of opportunity will not happen. Thus the classroom becomes a microcosm of the wider community and strategies to improve practice within it are seen to impact on the wider world:

> Transformation unfolds and is given structure by a consciousness of the whole. The task of transformation is to operate so that what we create grows organically, more concerned with the 'quality of aliveness' that gives us the experience of wholeness than with a predictable destination and a speed that with which we can reach it.
>
> An unfolding strategy requires giving an uncomfortable importance to each small step we take. We have to worry as much about the arrangement of a room as we do about the community that caused us to assemble . . . For example, each step of a master plan has to be a small example of the qualities we want in the final large thing. (Block, 2008, p. 20)

Dialogue on educational strategy and practice therefore needs to deepen in order to accommodate the needs of all through a shift of perspective. Those involved in children's learning will need to move away from the belief that the 'gifted' are at risk from the inclusion of 'others', and that inclusive practice can only happen through the accomplishment of 'superior' learners.

As outlined earlier, the thinking that creates barriers to inclusive practice derives from prejudice that is deeply-seated in teacher and practitioner attitudes:

> . . . the main barrier to inclusion lies in the teachers' perception that special children are different and that the task of educating them requires special expertise, special equipment, special training and special schools (e.g. Forlin 1995). Fortunately, the research evidence suggests that such attitudes often change once teachers have had direct experience of including such children in their classrooms. Nevertheless, teacher perceptions and attitudes present the most formidable obstacle to inclusion and cannot be ignored. (Mittler, 2004, p. 8)

Lack of experience will have a bearing on the attitudes of teachers and practitioners. In relation to disability, specifically, too few have worked with disabled children or indeed disabled colleagues, but there is equally less contact with different young people where communities are polarized and learners are divided. The barriers then arise from a school culture in which some children are believed to be 'talented' and others 'special', in which the deeper understanding of equality is shallow and poorly articulated in language and practice. As Gladwell explains:

This does not mean that when we are outside our areas of passion or experience our reactions are invariably wrong. It just means they are shallow. They are hard to explain and easily disrupted. They aren't grounded in real understanding. (Gladwell, 2005, p. 184)

Movement from a grade D to C is an achievement equal to movement from A to A*. In addition, meriting 'top' achievers alone impacts negatively on all learners, as it puts pressure and stress on high achievers to maintain their performance at the risk of losing status. (And, as we have said, such stresses easily cause mental illness, anxiety and depression.) At the same time, other learners (particularly those whose difference may mean the need to try harder) suffer the shame and humiliation of never being able to reach certain levels of attainment. In order to respect children's varied abilities, and work with them in new ways, teachers will need to know more about equality and diversity to robustly apply this to their teaching. It will mean that the school seeking to develop inclusive practice will view the curriculum and teaching not as dictators of outcomes but as enablers of growth.

This argument reinforces the rights dimension explored earlier. After all, a school that fails to tackle the culture that views inclusion as 'bringing faulty children up to standard' supports the implication that without 'them', the whole could function better. Clearly, classification on the basis of early academic attainment establishes patterns that fragment communities in later years. Social justice depends instead on very carefully considered change in systems and understanding. In the same way, by perpetuating special schooling, early years settings, schools, colleges and universities are allowed to avoid their responsibility to develop fairer practice (and ensuring happiness for all children) by accommodating only those children deemed 'normal' enough and ignoring those perceived as too different.

A culture of belonging

Meaningful relationships are built on trust, and they demand significant give and take. Establishing equality through inclusive practice requires that every teacher and practitioner must face up to the uneven power share in the classroom. Across schools, there is a need to challenge the idea that teachers 'give' a lesson. Schools need to demonstrate a different understanding about learning, one that is seen more as a dialogue in which adults and children share equally. Thus the interaction supports people's sense of belonging, one of mutual learning in which all participants grow to develop acceptance. The nurturing and caring culture that this demands is best exemplified in the following statement by the Early Childhood Forum:

Inclusion is a process of identifying, understanding and breaking down the barriers to participation and belonging. (Early Childhood Forum, 2003)

As we have seen, inclusive practice is characterized by developing new behaviours and strategies that uphold common values. It demands that meaningful, nurturing relationships are formed to encourage dialogue. Belonging implies a deeper connection than pure participation: effort is needed to engage each child, as well as the family and the wider community. Belonging is owned: it cannot be given or imposed and it requires a culture of shared leadership at every level of the organization:

> To know that I live in a community that cares about each and every one of us.
> Better praise if you get something right. (DCFS, 2008, p. 74)

Although a personal feeling may not be delivered or imposed, what teachers and practitioners say and the way that they organize their teaching have a serious impact on learners' sense of belonging. It is through the acceptance of teachers and peers that children derive that sense. To express acceptance, teachers and practitioners need to act in ways that tell learners that they are valued and wanted. Background, family circumstance and physical difference will have a bearing here. Furthermore, levels of understanding about equality also vary, so it is unfair to expect everyone to feel or act in similar ways, even in the same environment. However, taking young peoples' sense of belonging for granted and leaving it to chance is unacceptable, particularly given that teachers naturally hold more power within a relationship.

As our exploration of vulnerable children has underlined, difference has been perceived as problematic and this perspective is in itself divisive. For practice to become truly inclusive the emphasis must change: schools need to take a different approach to difference. As we have explained, organizational structures in schools are underpinned by some flawed ideologies that often interfere with relationships, impact on attitudes and affect growth. It therefore demands considered effort to actively and intentionally rethink practice and adjust behaviour so that communication is encouraged and belonging nurtured.

Within the context of the school, inclusive practice accepts that the starting point will differ for every child, and recognizes that different individuals, groups and communities will face different pressures. Clearly, then, inclusive practice demands a degree of complexity and will flex according to diverse individual needs and priorities.

Following, Carol Tashie clarifies the double-duty now imposed on schools that seek to implement educational change:

Inclusion is: All children belonging to the schools they would attend if they were not disabled AND support provided to children, families, and colleagues so that all can be successful. (Tashie, nd)

From a rights perspective, inclusive practice acknowledges that all children are entitled to belong to their local community schools. While developing a value-based approach is fundamental to nurturing children's resilience, the support of good relationships underpins their ability to flourish. Furthermore, social context and experience will determine our patterns of growth: equal opportunity to make contact with other young people is therefore vital. Without it there is a risk that some children will become isolated, and lose out on developing the new skills that only peers can teach. Peer mentoring supports social development in a way that adults cannot. In essence, nobody can teach an eight year old how to be eight – except another eight year old. In order to make friends each child needs to have met many other children in order to select those they like, so schools should recognize this and increase opportunity for contact within learning groups.

Belonging is not the same as having to join in. Neither does it mean that everybody must participate in every activity all the time. However, inclusive practice does demand the flexibility that enriches and enables young people's choice in learning. It also requires a willingness to respond by accommodating group and individual needs, while learning is taking place. Again the issue is not about what is right or wrong but about shared experience. For example, a university seeking to print all papers in one format and on one colour to suit all students misses the point. If practice reflects choice and flexibility, then offering different format, fonts and colours is far more likely to suit every student, with no need for compromise. Alternatively, a playgroup might change the rules of games on certain days to accommodate a child who thrives on higher levels of activity. At other times the rules may be left open so that the children can decide on what is fair or not, given their needs on the day. The point is that practice should accommodate to enable full participation all the time. It is then up to participants to choose how they want to join in.

Inclusive practice does not mean that you have to like each other, but that the culture should fully embrace difference and that all participants demonstrate this acceptance in their actions. True acceptance demands far more than lip service. Tolerance is the passive acknowledgement of difference; it is too shallow to convey meaningful intent to collaborate as equals. Tolerance fails to understand difference and avoids interaction that may, for some, feel raw and uncomfortable to begin with:

> When human intelligence and human goodness and affection are used together, all human actions become constructive. When we combine a warm heart with knowledge and education, we can learn to respect others' views and others' rights. (Dalai Lama and Cutler, 1998, p. 40)

So tolerance is only part of the answer. All children have an entitlement to the unconditional acceptance of their presence within their own communities. Furthermore, by being honest and open in our intent to understand each other, we can behave in a manner that demonstrates this unconditional acceptance. At the heart of acceptance and belonging we find the meaning of respect for each other:

> Respect also means honouring people's boundaries to the point of protecting them. If you respect someone, you do not intrude. At the same time, if you respect someone, you do not withhold yourself or distance yourself from them. I have heard many people claim that they were respecting someone by leaving them alone, when in fact they were simply distancing themselves from something they did not want to deal with. When we respect someone, we accept that they have things to teach us. (Isaacs, 1999, p. 114)

Inclusive practice does not mean that children's differences are denied, as this puts pressure on some to conform. Statements such as 'There's nothing wrong with her'; 'He can do it if he tries harder'; 'We treat you all the same' are hugely damaging. For some children it can be liberating to explain their behaviour and feelings with the help of a diagnosis or label. However, as we have outlined, labels used by teachers and practitioners to *categorize* can often lead to the stereotyping that may lead to false expectations based on assumptions.

Basic needs are similar, but they need to be met in diverse ways. Some will say that it is unfair if certain people are treated differently. However, if everyone receives the same treatment, the experience for each person is likely to be unfair. To create respectful environments, schools need to expand their definition of 'fairness' to mean 'everyone gets what they need (not necessarily what they want) to participate fully'. By applying this definition in practice, teachers and practitioners are much more likely to accommodate diversity and respect difference. At the most basic level, feeling accepted allows children to be themselves and to be open and honest about their needs.

9

Unity and community

Children's time in school is limited to term-time attendance throughout a few short years of their school-based lives. In order to make any significant change in society, the ideas outlined so far should therefore apply to their community participation and their understanding of lifelong learning. To be successful in changing, schools need to find ways to mitigate these divides by providing opportunities beyond the school gates that foster cross-generation relationships and learning.

Population intervention is an intentional strategy that involves families and the wider community in improving the wellbeing of the whole community. It is a chance to apply the ideas we have described in order to breakdown the barriers created by the school organization. Ultimately, community learning can enable young people to enjoy and progress through meaningful contribution to their local communities. If people are to reassess their views on sharing resources and implement change, then it is vital that they understand population change. Social change will take place irrespective of intervention but purposeful action catalyses the process. Thus, by involving communities, schools can share the load and have greater impact.

In this chapter we look at collaboration and competition in terms of achievement and gratification. The reason people engage in specific activities is that they enjoy doing them. Doing something for the love of it and finding others with whom to share passion gives meaning beyond monetary reward. People gain from joining a community that shares their interest because it validates the activity, inspires and innovates, creating energy that is both gratifying **and** sustainable.

The development of community projects and local activities is a logical application of the theories outlined so far. Opportunities for work involving local groups enable children to gain an understanding of the community structure and social contribution that are so vital to wellbeing. These concepts underpin the route to Seligman's 'meaningful life' which gives children a greater sense of purpose and continuity. This sense of belonging contributes to children's sense of worth and identity: Robinson (2009) calls this 'finding one's tribe'. This association is more than simple affiliation: it is about contribution and the discovery of shared purpose and gratification in activities that benefit others.

To understand shared capacity demands an appreciation of the discrimination and stereotype pressures discussed in Chapter 4. It also implies a drive to take proactive action to diminish them. To explain this and enable fair and positive change we look at Baron-Cohen's (Goldenfield et al., 2005) 'system–empathy continuum', and Seligman's ideas on *virtues* to help us to move beyond passive understanding towards practical solutions.

Population intervention

Community involvement is the ideal way for schools to apply our real-world ideas, addressing inequality in their local area. They can identify the pressures, outline a strategy for change and take action to change the lives of the individual child, the family and the whole community.

Culture impacts on equity by influencing outcomes, so addressing wider community concerns will improve personal perception and circumstance. Programmes intended to enrich the environment for whole communities will ultimately improve the lives of those within the school. The school's culture both reflects and influences its community. Although visions will differ depending on the needs of each community group, the purpose of greater equality for all needs to remain the focus.

Certain principles will help to achieve this:

- Wellbeing is fundamentally about human rights: all people have a fundamental entitlement to sharing in and contributing to their community.
- Belonging to the group, contributing to progress and reaching a collective vision through dialogue are paramount.
- There are no right or wrongs and no perfect solutions. The outcomes are no more important than the process of working together.
- Applying virtues through strength define the movement: it is a journey not a target.

The p*opulation* defined in this context is the part of the community with which the school has a relationship – parents, siblings, neighbours or members from local associations – and therefore can influence its community. *Intervention* here means sharing the knowledge and skills that help increase individual wellbeing and applying these ideas to programmes and strategies that benefit the wider community. In this way, what is done differently tackles inequality head on and thereby has a direct impact on the factors affecting the wellbeing of the local community.

This does not mean that schools provide 'family' lessons in wellbeing or in social justice *per se*, but that schools offer opportunities to share in the activities that shape community transformation. Intervention is not restricted to informing: participants develop wellbeing by applying ideas and identifying the principles and values that underpin them:

> The school actively engages and listens to parents, fathers as well as mothers, and works with them as partners in their children's learning and development. (Department for Children, Schools and Families, 2008, p. 12)

There is little point addressing the environment within the school if it contrasts with its local community. Buildings and systems are arbitrary limits that contain the group defined as 'school': all group members are connected to the wider community through a rich web of overlapping and interconnected relationships. Members of a group will also be members of many others. However, the environment is a *shared* concern, so it is important is to find a place where all members can unite to improve it. Here begins a dialogue, where members have an equal say in the issues to be addressed, the direction of change and the local action required.

A community approach to population intervention makes sense for the following reasons:

1. It addresses uneven resourcing by funding strategies that benefit the whole community, not just those groups identified as 'needy'.
2. It provides an alternative to marginalizing practice and thus reduces the stress on those worst affected without hindering those who flourish.

Numerous projects and activities may help to encourage participation and reduce inequality. They include adult learning programmes, classes shared with members of other institutions and family activity sessions within the school. What's more, participation in learning activities that benefit the wider community are rewarding in themselves. They also introduce people from the local area into the school and involve them in change.

The outcomes of such programmes should address issues identified by participants from the community. As we have stated, control is critical and, unless power is explicitly conferred, imbalances will persist. In order to articulate the principle of equality the school needs to support the issues of greatest concern to local associations and not dictate to them. Shared goals should be allowed to emerge, avoiding any perceptions that motives and agendas are imposed or directed.

Children are only at school for about 15 per cent of the year, so without the opportunity to apply what they have learned, their skills and knowledge risk being lost (Gladwell, 2008). Ideally, the ongoing support of friends and family along with the provision of suitable community programmes will keep learning active (and the school community alive) whether young people are in or out of class. Community programmes are therefore not only critical to learning but they avoid losing term-time learning. In addition, finding a use for school buildings and equipment makes good sense when they benefit the community that ultimately funds them through taxes. Even in the absence of these wider benefits, evidence shows that pupils engaged in gratifying activities such as music, study or sport report higher wellbeing scores. (Ironically, however, Seligman (2002) finds that they view those who hang around streets and shops as having more fun.) If these strategies also improve academic standards, they are worth undertaking, but if there are tangible benefits for local communities then the social outcomes alone are worth considering.

As we have seen, addressing those worst affected by inequality is of the highest priority. Intervention needs to be centred on delivering specific skills to enable choice, control and increased opportunity to participate. Given good opportunities to contribute, people are better able to make the right choices for themselves and act in ways that benefit others. Population intervention at a community level is probably the best antidote to the pressures created by modern living as it enables people to give. By changing old habits, new ones that promote shared activity can appear.

Huppert (2005) explains that people become more skilled in achieving wellbeing when they behave and think in new ways. Such new habits may make the difference between a person flourishing and developing mental illness. The same theory can be applied to whole groups and wider communities. For thriving communities, insight into the impact of such behaviour change is crucial. It adds to the need for developing joint activity, sharing new understanding and establishing new norms. If the joint activity in question has other benefits (such as creating a community garden or a shared allotment) then there is value both for the individual and the community By introducing whole groups to ways of working and the understanding that furthers wellbeing, every member will benefit.

The wider the intervention the more effective the resulting change. Population intervention can contribute to the wellbeing of the most vulnerable (in Figure 9.1 these are the individuals under extreme stress). In short, applying wider strategies for positive change across communities can shift the mean and avoid the antisocial behaviour associated with those at the left-hand side of the population spectrum. The following extract on alcohol consumption illustrates how this process works:

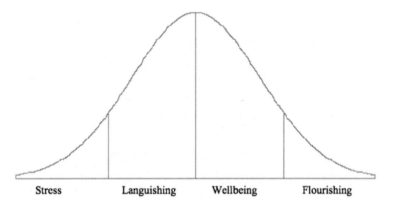

Stress   Languishing   Wellbeing   Flourishing

Figure 9.1 Psychological dispositions across the population.

> They concluded that a small reduction in the mean consumption of light or
> moderate drinkers (for example, by increasing the cost of alcohol or discouraging
> binge drinking) is likely to result in a substantial decrease in serious alcohol-related
> problems. This conclusion follows from the fact that there is essentially a normal
> distribution of alcohol consumption in the population and, for normal distribution,
> when there is a small shift in the mean, there is a large shift in the tails of the
> distribution. Rose (1992, p. 64) has suggested that, in a similar manner, deviant
> behaviours such as violence are 'simply the tail of the population's own
> distribution'. Therefore, reducing the mean level of violence or the mean of its
> risk factors in a population should reduce the prevalence of serious violence and
> related crime. (Huppert *et al.*, 2005, p. 327)

Similarly, widening learning programmes to those outside the school will further
increase the positive factors and decrease the negative factors that influence all
children. While the aim is to quickly remove the factors affecting those most at risk, all
members of the school will benefit from the new ways of working. The outcomes are
positive across the population, school and community. The numbers of those who
already flourish will increase, alongside those who enjoy moderate wellbeing. More
significantly, the number of those languishing will decrease, and those facing extreme
stress could disappear altogether over time (see Figure 9.2).

Most significantly, nobody loses out through population intervention: as the shaded
area shows in Figure 9.2, when wellbeing increases for an entire population, the most
significant change is with the decrease in numbers is for those who were experiencing
extreme stress. Therefore, interventions can help move the whole population along the
wellbeing continuum by working with all participants. This demonstrates that
programmes with community participation have greatest impact, and will enable a
greater number of children and adults to flourish.

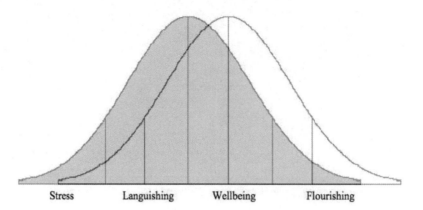
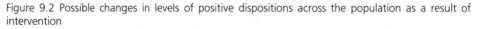

| Stress | Languishing | Wellbeing | Flourishing |

Figure 9.2 Possible changes in levels of positive dispositions across the population as a result of intervention

By developing alternative ways of working with various groups of people across different local associations, schools can facilitate shared learning across traditional divides. For example, parents who continue to act as reading buddies after their own children have left the school can become peer mentors for younger parents. When adults are actively engaged in the community, connections thrive and equality of status challenges the *professional* superiority often accorded to specific, hierarchical paid roles. Working on an equal footing with people from the local area will demand the development of new skills, which can only add value to the school.

Collaboration

One of those skills is the ability to work collaboratively. Teachers and practitioners will need to work with, learn from and appreciate the contribution of an increasing number of people from very different backgrounds without feeling threatened. The argument here acknowledges that competition can be worthwhile provided that it avoids disempowering others. More fundamentally, however, we should question whether a culture that upholds competition does in fact value the contribution from all those who participate in the school. Do communities gain from competition? Ultimately this is about regaining fairness and levelling the playing field, so that competition exists only for the common good. The ideas explored with reference to culture change and inclusive practice need to be extended across the limits of school organization and structure.

Low status dissuades individuals from contributing to the wider good, but the development of collaborative, cross-organizational learning programmes can help to counter competition and consumerism.

Competition? The driving force behind capitalism and sport and technical progress? I know. But think about it this way. Competition between people ensures only one thing: that if you win, you will have done a *better* job at whatever it is than the other person did. That does not mean that you will have done a *good* job, just a better one. To compete does not ensure certain excellence. It just ensures comparative success. (Kline, 1999, p. 71)

Cooperation, on the other hand, demands an appreciation that the ultimate goal is to better the game for all the participants. Being better than the next class, group or school does not necessarily benefit the wider community. In a system where the standards and targets are a measure of competition, there is little imperative to do things differently. Contrary to popular belief, team experiments show that the drive for higher results actively *discourages* team members from engaging in collaborative behaviours. This in turn stifles effort (Dweck, 2006). It means that, although specified individual targets might be achieved, the culture may prevent the mutual development and innovation inspired by collaborative team working. The outcomes of egotistical competition are reflected in our current social concerns as the inability to gain gratification from shared outcomes – divided communities, the reporting of crime and violence, squandered resources, and climate change.

The thing that will help [keep] me healthy, happy and safe is we get along well in the environment and we should not be against each other but work as a team and do our best to the people our age that need help. (DCFS, 2007a, p. 75)

All participants within schools need to understand these subtleties in order to engage effectively with people in their local communities. At a time when standards are being redefined, schools need to grasp the nettle and use their unique position to influence what is measured and where gains are made.

Community learning

While children need the support of good relationships with teachers and peers, they should also understand the importance of a connection with the wider community. Social relationships, mentoring and peer coaching are often pivotal in helping young people to recognize their strengths and how to use them. Most importantly, adults can often help children find their sense of purpose: through conversations and shared activity children learn about accepted values and the strength of applied virtue. Individuals do have to fit into their society and abide by its accepted values.

Fortunately, society in general is moving away from assigning blame, by reason of moral character, to groups on the basis of individual characteristics and personal preference:

> The doctrine of good character had teeth as the ideological engine for a host of nineteenth-century social institutions. Much of insanity was seen as moral degeneracy and defect, and 'moral' treatment (the attempt to replace bad character with virtue) was its dominant kind of therapy. The temperance movement, woman's suffrage, child labour laws, and radical abolitionist are even more important outgrowths. (Seligman, 2002, p. 125)

Society has begun to recognize that the way certain groups miss out and the prejudice they face do more to jeopardize their wellbeing. This understanding is key to addressing the attitudes and systems threatening the lives of those most stifled, and transforming society's oppressive culture:

> So social evidence lets us escape from the value-laden, blame accruing, religious inspired, class-oppressing notion of character and get on with the monumental task of building a healthier 'nurturing' environment. (ibid., p. 127)

A social approach further strengthens the need for population intervention to focus strategies and resources, to address inequalities and eradicate individual blame. Such strategies need to be implemented, enhancing the lives of all those avoiding the perception that resources are being used by one group at the expense of another:

> If wellbeing reflects the goals for human life, it must include not only the subjective dimensions of happiness and flourishing mental health but also the objective, pro-social motivation and ability to make positive contributions to the lives others. Combining these subjective and objective dimensions, we define well-being as *thriving lives*, the conditions of lives that are good for both the individual and for society. (Ashcroft and Carrowe, 2005, p. 1)

Schools need to set up the conditions in which children can learn and develop the skills needed to make the right choices for their whole community. This demands that schools work with families and develop an appreciation of what contributes to wellbeing so that the benefits can be appreciated, measured and celebrated. In its simplest sense, wellbeing should be a shared concern which is culturally relevant and encompasses individual health, social relationships and community welfare.

Finding meaning beyond the school

It is notable that the *Good Childhood Report* saw 'positive contribution to economic wellbeing' as being least relevant to children. This disparity may arise from the widening relevance gap between school studies and real-life jobs. In the long run our communities need people who can contribute both to the wealth and lives of others. According to Baron-Cohen (Goldenfield et al., 2005) people can be categorized along a continuum from systemizer to empathizer, with men tending to lean towards systemizing and women empathizing:

> Two key modes of thought are systemizing and empathizing (Baron-Cohen, 2002). Systemizing is the drive to understand rules governing the behaviour of systems and the drive to construct systems that are lawful. Systemizing allows one to predict and control such systems. Empathizing is the drive to identify another person's thoughts or emotions, and to respond to emotional states with an appropriate emotion. Empathizing allows one to predict another person's behaviour at a level that is accurate enough to facilitate social interaction. (Goldenfield et al., 2005, p. 338)

It is not that systems are wrong in themselves, for categorization and order are extremely useful in the right context. However, given that there are two ends to this continuum and that most people will be placed in-between rather than be polarized, balance is vital. In short, an empathetic approach should be equally valued, although this is not currently the case.

In fact, community work is particularly ill-suited to a systematic structure. The chain of command imposed by the organizational tree corrodes the culture of contribution that feeds community energy. As people come together in partnership, a web of deeply enmeshed connections can develop that rarely follows any logical sequence. From the social justice perspective in particular, the passion fuelling community action is born out of empathy – a desire to right wrong: to fight for justice, love, humanity and harmony with wisdom, courage and knowledge. These virtues, described by Seligman (2005) as internationally ubiquitous (i.e. valued by virtually every culture) need to be promoted and celebrated. They may be deeply unfashionable in an era where high performance and celebrity status generate vast press coverage, but they may need to be reinstated. They need to be valued and shared as a way of gaining happiness – not in a moralistic way but as a choice on the path to self-fulfilment.

When empathy is valued, it gives individuals more ways of contributing to their communities. Many of these require no cash – they are quite simply 'the things money cannot buy'. Unfortunately, caring and giving are recognized as belonging to the female domain, when in fact the qualities should be celebrated in any individual. In *The Female Advantage*, Helgesen (1995) describes the successful relationship-building qualities women bring to their jobs: their willingness to share information and a wider sense of identity (focusing on the world rather than just the institution) which was strengthened by their participation in extra-employment activities. The words they used (flow, interaction, access, involvement, network) emphasize activity undertaken in shared relationships with others.

> The female view that one strengthens self by strengthening others is finding greater acceptance. As Miller states, this approach to leadership is precisely what is needed to address the alienation that troubles our public institutions – business, politics, medicine and the law. We need leaders who can work against alienation by bridging the gap between demands of efficiency and the need to nurture the human spirit. (Helgesen, 1995, pp. 233–4)

Complex relationships may be intertwined but they remain rich and important elements of community work. They characterize interdependence in which people share power and take responsibility easily, and they foster the trust and acceptance that empower people to reach out beyond their boundaries.

Liberating cultures

When people are not paid to do specific work they do it for very different motives. In this sense the term '*amateur*', translated from French (Latin in origin) to the English '*lover of*', reflects a voluntary motivation to work as a result of personal passion for a particular activity.

Without official professional status, people's contribution is often perceived as inferior when in fact it may be wholly worthwhile. Pay and positions muddy the waters, reducing outcomes to materialistic values and robbing individuals and communities of greater benefits. Working towards a common goal creates respect within cultures and can build trust in a community. Community programmes are no magical solution and building relationships takes time. Initial meetings are often poorly attended but, as word spreads and benefits are felt, interest and engagement tend to grow.

Figure 9.3 shows the change in the relationships within a group over time: people gain confidence in their strengths and raise their contribution. In the early stages, people may not feel that they are equals and may fear rejection by the group. They

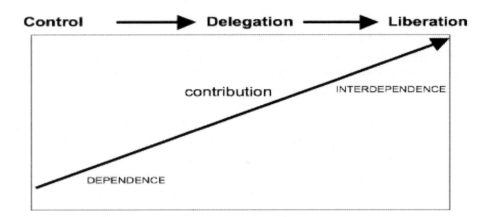

Figure 9.3 How interdependence enhances engagement

may struggle to find a sense of belonging. Some will find it difficult to understand the value of establishing connections beyond their normal hierarchy and environment. Individuals may need to assert personal power in order to feel in control. Others might feel dependent and defer to others rather than take the lead in their own learning. Unless those categorized by a paid position make an intentional effort to change the way they work, the power balance in the early stages is likely to be skewed.

As the relationships within communities mature, role differences become less distinct, and members assume greater individual responsibility for the shared work. In reaching a joint understanding of interdependence, each person's behaviour will have changed to maintain the community values. New work will develop as a social activity. The links and personal development that arise are valued not only by individuals but also by the wider community.

Time and budgets are finite. If the overarching goal is to seek wholeness, then it is essential to identify resources and strengths within relationships and across existing groups. Communities can function better as a whole if connection to *all* parts are strong – even the weaker ones! It is far better for weaker members to work towards a shared goal than to abdicate responsibility or work against it. Furthermore, if our weaknesses are perceived as areas needing development they are more likely to be valued and sustained by the whole. In this way they are no longer perceived as problematic but are part of greater success.

Child development thrives on peer coaching and mentoring. Not only do good relationships provide support and enjoyment in learning but they also offer opportunities for modelling and reinforcement in mixed ability groups.

In the following example, envisage 'the weeds' as divisive thinking and discriminatory behaviour.

To give you an analogy for building capacity we can think of a lawn. My Dad's lawn is very beautiful with densely packed grass, evenly mowed in stripes. And my Dad has plenty of advice about how this can be achieved by anyone. 'What you have to do', says my Dad, 'is to feed it regularly during the growing season and make sure that it is well aerated by putting holes in it with a fork. If you do this then the grass will grow better and will out-compete all the other species and you won't have to worry about weeding. In fact the lawn becomes so thick that it becomes resistant to weeds because the seeds that fall on it struggle to take root and fail to grow. In fact if you have a good lawn then it is very little work indeed.' Thanks Dad. And that's what building capacity is about, the idea that we move forwards faster and more easily if we can build on what people can do rather than focusing on their problems. (Mundy, 2007)

We can apply this thinking to people within our communities: perceiving everybody as valuable raises overall expectation. Changing our behaviour to help build capacity increases the likelihood of success, which in turn increases motivation and commitment to positive change. Achievement and fulfilment promote personal morale as well as an ethos of belonging, loyalty and collaboration within and between teams. The more an organization works with the community it serves, the more people will feel valued, safe and wanted. A shared approach to developing new meaning enables all community members to grow together in strength and confidence.

Relationships: developing respect for 'childhood'

As previously identified, one of the most positive sources of wellbeing is the sense that one is part of a community. For children this surely should mean a period of privilege, not purely a period of training for adulthood where rights are somewhat diminished by the nature of their status. Many have pointed to the fact that the effect of consumerism on our social view of children has led to a double standard that erodes their value in a significant way. Children's place in the community is marginalized because we see them as consumers, not contributors. What they bring is ignored and their participation is further marginalized, creating divides that impoverish the experience for all concerned:

Humans have a long period of development – from infancy through puberty – we depend strongly on others. Even as adults we function much better when we are embedded in social networks that offer cooperation, support and enjoyment. (Diener and Biswas-Diener, 2008, p. 50)

Children and young people need their family, friends and community to celebrate their place in a flourishing community. To belong to a community demands more than just a physical presence: we each need to feel that our uniqueness is unconditionally accepted.

Peer understanding is an important key to improvement and growth. Inevitably, pupil culture will differ from staff culture in school. No matter how much effort is put into managing children's relationships, adult influence (however well-intentioned) can only be peripheral. Young people will inevitably create their own rules, language and shared understanding. But, without adults to enable and offer opportunities for peer learning, young people will not benefit from their own strengths and abilities:

> First and foremost, other people allow us to love and be loved. They help us feel secure and cared for; they value us and will step up to the plate for us if we need help. At the same time, loving other people gives us an opportunity to grow and enlarge ourselves. Further, when we take pride in the accomplishments of others, and they take pride in ours, we then share deep bond. (Diener and Biswas-Diener, 2008, p. 54)

If education continues to foster a culture where only high performance is valued, then it will do so at the cost of an ever-widening attainment gap. This cost seems not only high but also outdated in the context of our present service economy, where the ability to respond to others individually is highly sought by employers. A high-achievement focus may expand, assess and classify learners' heads, but it ignores their needs as people within communities where collaboration is critical. Relationships are not only a route to other skills or a fortunate by-product of school life; they are centrally important to effective learning:

> An inclusive approach is **no less** concerned with achievements but with all the achievements of all children and young people, and with the meaning of achievements within communities. An inclusive approach is equally concerned with learning, but instead of focusing on outcomes gives **equal** attention to the conditions for teaching and learning, so that the resources and relationships that support the active and sustained involvement of children, families and practitioners in education are maintained. (Ainscow and Dyson, 2006, p. 29)

Developing respect within groups is central: we cannot impose friendships, but we can develop cultures in which individuals value each other's perspectives and uniqueness. If shared understanding is to emerge from good practice, then friendship must be valued as beneficial, not incidental. Where a culture reflects equality and inclusion is embodied in policy and systems, respect will flourish. However the reverse is also true.

Naturally, we would expect to see change at all types of levels as a result of community engagement. But what are the new measures of success? If the meaning and outcome of our work have changed, then so will the measures of their success. New scales must be developed to quantify how successfully we put values into practice within our communities.

The task demands careful thought. If we pursue reflective action in the development of change and impact on culture, then how should we assess the outcomes? What new behaviours reflect the values that we seek to achieve?

At a personal level, development leads to empowerment and raises learner confidence to pursue ideas whether alone or in a group. Perhaps we can find ways to measure personal effectiveness with regard to personal meaning and shared understanding:

- What did I do differently?
- What have I learned?
- What can I share?

At a group level, this might mean becoming more effective at sharing skills, welcoming new members or supporting more diverse community members by developing strategies and processes.

At the wider community level we would expect greater participation from increasingly diverse sectors. We would wish to monitor and assess links between schools, colleges, universities, community groups, private and public sector organizations and other associates working towards shared visions and outcomes.

From the very beginning, people need to be purposeful about creating fresh paths and putting aside their usual practice to create something new. The intention must be clear. The aim is to create community work that will challenge existing rules and, through working together, enable new outcomes for people. Existing community divisions are removed, allowing people to develop and participate more fully. Positive and supportive community processes are central to such development. New groups and communication channels reveal connections between people that do not ordinarily operate together. Roles and positions are challenged. Personal power is set aside in favour of achieving the greater, joint objectives. The community decides how to learn together, to build resources, support change, draw on what people bring and challenge expectation. It is in this context that equality and equity, and so social justice, are most likely to flourish in practical and meaningful ways.

10 The adult team

Introduction

This chapter explores how the adults within education and children's services can develop ideas that promote wellbeing by working as 'the adult team'. Contributing to a more respectful environment should ultimately deliver personal satisfaction and shared appreciation. Ongoing teamwork is an ideal application for our ideas and practices on raising wellbeing in the school community. The way adults work together need to reflect an appreciation that shared responsibility strengthens social justice. Furthermore, when children see adults questioning the *status quo* and resolving inequality, it shows them that values are important and that change can be achieved by changing practice rather than simply remembering theory. Lessons in social justice or equality are somewhat meaningless if the adults around children engage in unfair practice: the adult team, therefore, may want to work towards greater fairness if learning is to have impact. Adults need to model social justice in practice – the effective team is a powerful model of equality and equity at work.

This chapter also provides an opportunity to review ideas from an adult perspective. By doing so, they can improve their participation in lifelong learning and contribute to a deeper *learning culture*. We examine the school's adult team as a microcosm of society, and question how individual understanding of these ideas has wider implications for us all. As a living entity made up from classes, departments and groups, the whole school exemplifies the delicate relationships that exist between individual, group, nation and planet.

In effective teams, each member combines a high degree of autonomy and specialization. Each role, however small, is indispensable to shared progress. Every individual is able to bring a unique contribution to themselves and the group, enabling movement towards a common goal. The building blocks of team wellbeing should also raise individual contributions to personal flourishing and a thriving school. We also look at the role of passion and excitement in problem solving. When change is understood and progress is appreciated, individual work is more pleasurable. Furthermore, when people move together in step, they generate enthusiasm and share satisfaction.

A moral basis for change

Deliberate mistreatment within teams is unfair and directly hurtful to certain individuals but, in general, inequalities are more subtle and prompt more generalized languishing that impacts negatively on everyone. In some schools the adult team clearly includes everyone working within the school. However, in others a boundary persists between teaching and non-teaching staff, inter-agency professionals and community workers. Adult hierarchies can be imposed by designated specialism, sector, subject or rank. The majority of schools will vary between rigid structures and more flexible ways of working, but in some the pecking order is very clearly defined. For example, teaching assistants will not attend staff meetings or may not be made welcome in the staff room.

The problem is that individual responsibility for unfair treatment can often be abandoned: blame is attached to school organization or lack of government direction. In some cases, the issue is simply ignored. When this happens the status quo survives and no-one questions those who suffer as a result. This means that adult contributions are treated unequally, since only a number of adults are perceived as *teachers*. There are consequences here for tackling or ignoring inequality, and the identification of those deemed responsible for striving towards social justice. In fact, if *social justice* is seen as a subject to be taught, then teachers are merely responsible for passing on information about inequality, and reform activity is then perceived as beyond the school's remit. In such cases, responsibility could be understood as belonging to a role, *wellbeing officers*, whose job description includes the implementation of appropriate changes. However, the pursuit of wellbeing is both a personal and shared concern requiring *everyone's* engagement and accountability – so full involvement is essential.

The prevailing hierarchy generally favours seniority or academic status and this has practical implications for schools. For example, the head of an English department is more likely to have a say in decisions concerning literacy strategies than a parent 'reading buddy' or a teaching assistant, when in fact they may have more personal and creative solutions for supporting a weaker reader who they know and understand. Such unequal opportunity clearly limits fair involvement and contribution from all members of the adult team. As the following suggests, such practice is detrimental to adult wellbeing:

> Those perceived as other within the team often feel alienated and consequently limit or reserve their contribution (Milliken and Martins, 1996). The habitual response to stress is fight or flight, and therefore, not surprisingly, research indicates greater conflict and turnover amongst diverse teams (Dreaschlin et al., 2000). (Lumby with Coleman, 2007, p. 115)

The cost of inequality can be high in terms of resources wasted through lack of adult engagement. If an individual feels pressurized to compete or compromise in order to gain respect or acceptance, they stop wanting to give. For example, a parent who might have felt happy to organize and supervise an after-school activity club might pull out if he or she feels that his or her contribution will not be appreciated. The wider effect on the whole adult team is negative: when the value of one's contribution is perceived as dependent status or paid role, other members will be less inclined to take initiative or participate. Any adult hierarchy is divisive because where role defines status; contribution is usually limited to the activities defined by a job description. However, contributing to wellbeing often requires adults to break the bounds of their job description. Therefore, everyone is in a position to contribute to the adult team's learning, when a great deal of thought and deliberate action is required. When addressing inequality the specific action sometimes needed demands both skill and will to make the right moral journey: this may involve an acknowledgement of qualities such as kindness, care and empathy. In other words, tackling inequality requires that every voice is given equal value, so that shared thinking can contribute to shared wisdom – the skill and will to change.

Systemic discrimination and human rights

The narrower the parameters for success, the more uneven is the learning and the more limiting and inhibiting the school culture. Whatever the scope or nature of the discrimination, a culture that seeks only the narrowest and most rigid outcomes is inevitably prejudiced and this in turn inhibits the emergence of many qualities that are invaluable to learning. Passion, playfulness and humanity may be the very qualities that make the adult team successful and inspire each member to improve, but they must be recognized – or lost. Thus a narrow academic focus may cost the loss of talented members of the adult team when even the best become dissatisfied with their relative invisibility and seek employment elsewhere.

Without the development of practices that increase fairer opportunities for employment, fair pay and a non-discriminatory environment, members of the adult team have little chance of equally developing the skills that support their own wellbeing. Schools may lack the influence on wider social problems, but they need to continually address issues of fairness within their own teams. As outlined in Chapter 8 with respect to inclusive practice, addressing the teaching culture in the same way is a continuing endeavour. Anything less is a breach of the following human rights:

> Human rights: Article 23.
> (1) Everyone has the right to work, to free choice of employment, to just and favourable conditions of work and to protection against unemployment.
> (2) Everyone, without any discrimination, has the right to equal pay for equal work.
> (3) Everyone who works has the right to just and favourable remuneration ensuring for himself and his family an existence worthy of human dignity, and supplemented, if necessary, by other means of social protection.
> (4) Everyone has the right to form and to join trade unions for the protection of his interests. (United Nations, 2009)

Defining systemic discrimination is doubly difficult in a culture where intelligence levels are regarded as fixed and where ranking is therefore seen as a predictor of performance and result. Furthermore, when status is determined on a single continuum, personal capacity is reduced to a nominal level of ability. As previously identified, the higher the ranking, the more pronounced the effects of hierarchy on personal status and self-esteem. There is also a tendency for those at most disadvantage within the system to rationalize their lack of current ability by accepting and internalising inadequacy rather than challenging the effects of hierarchy.

Research shows that while some people are hesitant about stating outright that they experience discrimination, they can often describe how they had been treated unfairly or put in difficult situations (Lumby with Coleman, 2007). For example, in schools where teaching assistants are excluded from the dialogue that could improve practice they are more likely to have a difficult relationship with other teachers than get dissatisfied with the way the school is organized and the accepted 'lower status'. In other words, people often find it more difficult to articulate the social cause of discrimination, and easier to describe the personal results of prejudice without identifying the cause. This hinders a viable solution: internalizing the problem reinforces a belief in personal deficit and in addition removes any sense obligation to those most advantaged by the system – something of a double whammy! This also explains why pointing out the unfair advantage is often ill received by those who feel they deserve their privileged position and perceive it as blame, which does little to improve culture.

Preventing bullying by tackling prejudice

Just as we urged that the most vulnerable children should be supported first, so adults may need to tackle the most difficult inequalities first. Life circumstances mean that adult team members face numerous pressures and their wellbeing is often compromised. While those in the most difficult circumstances require the most urgent support, no member need be identified as vulnerable or at risk. Those under most stress can do without the embarrassment or becoming the target for blame.

Building capacity that embraces a shared understanding of systemic discrimination is therefore essential so that team members understand the personal benefits of addressing inequality's underlying causes. Furthermore, addressing the issue from a whole team perspective also means that those in less demanding roles, those who are consistently better off as a result of having less to deal with, are more likely to participate. This has great significance considering the power shifts that may need addressing within the adult team and the feeling that can engender:

> Rather than the ubiquitous normative assumption that educational leaders are committed to equity, a political perspective would suggest that any attempts to redistribute power, to disturb current relations, will be met with resistance, hostility, and retaliation. (Lumby with Coleman, 2007, p. 80)

Ultimately, shared accountability is key to minimizing these negative feelings and resolving the issues of assumed unfairness caused to a few in the short term. Where the adult team can work together to identify the pressures on its members (environmental, physical, social and organizational), it will be in a better position to accept change.

To add to the complexity, while culture can be tackled within the school the adult team can do little about external social pressures. It is therefore critical that all team members are involved in defining the factors for the school's improvement. Any adult left out of this process will be unable to support colleagues or acknowledge the added pressure he or she may face. So it is important that the increased effort by some members of the adult team is acknowledged, particularly when dealing with feelings of hostility as discussed above. Otherwise, false assumptions become entrenched when the stereotypes are allowed to persist and people's capabilities are underestimated. For blame to be minimized, the need for change needs to be seen as important to all adults and a part of a wider drive for long-term school improvement. Here again, balance is important:

> As much as we all despise racism and sexism, these isms have only recently been considered moral turpitudes, and thus condemning Thomas Jefferson for keeping slaves or Sigmund Freud for patronising women is a bit like arresting someone today for having driven without a seatbelt in 1923. (Gilbert, 2006, p. 146)

Achieving fair practice immediately is impossible and would demand great change too quickly: after all, seatbelts were not introduced overnight. Although profound changes do need time, a degree of haste and sustained effort are important to keep things moving and secure those required most urgently. Just as seatbelts are now the norm, so too will society reject the many forms of discrimination that currently obstruct inclusive practice.

Above all, the acknowledgement of the importance and benefits of change brings flexibility. As 'common sense', misogyny and racial exploitation are re-evaluated, prior prejudice will disappear only where they are challenged. Ignorance and prejudice can be tackled more rapidly by reflective and proactive learning: schools therefore need urgently to tackle the relevant inconsistencies in adult understanding.

Orientation and practical wisdom

To have effective change, it is not enough to define inequality: each team member must also travel eagerly in the same direction. It is also critical for each to know what other team members gain from participation so that plans are shared and contributions are appreciated. Successful and diverse teams working across schools and services will need a broad understanding of individual roles and shared goals. With team members seeking various outcomes, different motivations also need to be appreciated and their place in change acknowledged.

It is crucial that members understand the importance of individual effort: discovering other people's stories and wishes plays an important part in teamwork. Cleaners may not do *everything* that heads do, but they do *everything* cleaners do, and without them the school would be a mess. Jobs are rarely identical, and even various individuals doing the same jobs will do them in different ways. There is no right way, but there can be common purpose when every team member can contribute uniquely to team effort. In the flourishing school everyone plays a unique part in the overall success, using their knowledge and skills. In other words, cleaners can have as much impact on wellbeing as headteachers. For example, toilet areas are renowned for some children as unsafe places because of the taunting they receive there from others. A cleaner, aware of this, may be able to turn the situation around by being present at break times, providing attractive soap and flowers, and making a risky place safer and more pleasant. These exemplars of practical wisdom rarely feature as a duty on the job description, but they have a major impact on wellbeing within the school.

There are certain features in the way people perceive their work that enable some to go beyond their basic job description duties. Human interaction, moral judgement and the wider social implications associated with the work make the difference. Diener and Biswas-Diener (2008) articulate this difference as a person's mode of orientation towards their work. There are three types of orientation, *job*, *career* and *calling*. While no one person will be one or the other, understanding how they relate and motivate could be a major step towards generating greater satisfaction a person gets from work.

Job orientation is characterized by a greater personal motivation for money, with the adult team member gaining little satisfaction from the work *per se*. Instead they watch the clock and see the job as a means to an end. This type of person would be unlikely to be a positive role model to children, since, as we have seen, money combined with a failure to enjoy and engage in work rarely brings happiness in the long term.

Career-oriented members might enjoy their work but they are motivated by advancement. This tends to lead to social comparison and therefore dissatisfaction. The career-oriented individual sets out to impress, working hard for promotion and external validation. The career-orientated team member reinforces ideas of hierarchy, and would teach children that competition and advancement are acceptable. As we have seen, such social comparison threatens happiness and fuels inequality.

Calling-orientated team members are most likely to want to apply ideas to their own lives and their job roles that nurture and sustain wellbeing. They are people who enjoy most aspects of their work. They are motivated to contribute to wider issues and find work so enjoyable they think about it after work hours. They find work rewarding and they work hard because they find their job meaningful. As Diener explains:

> People with a calling orientation usually love their jobs. They feel like their work is important, and makes a contribution to the world. They are excited and challenged by their daily work … Calling-orientated people are not workaholics; they are passionate workers who believe in what they do. (Diener and Biswas-Diener, 2008, p. 70)

If, within the adult team, members are able to identify the elements of their daily activities that suit a *calling* orientation, they may be more likely to find purpose and gratification in their work. Calling activities add to motivation and stimulate enjoyment, thus adding meaning and value to their individual contribution. With this in mind, the adult team members might need to work together to redefine job descriptions in order to identify activities that make the greatest contribution to wider social goals (this might mean new roles for some – possibly outside the school). In this way, criteria for personal achievement are broadened and people are enabled to participate more fully.

As Schwartz and Sharpe (2006) explain, job descriptions often fall short of articulating the dimension of practical wisdom:

> ... in addition to skill, which is what the intellectual strengths contribute to, practical wisdom requires will. To be wise, it is not enough to know the right thing to do. You also have to want to do it. In the absence of will, the intellectual and emotional skills that make up practical wisdom can be used as instruments of manipulation and abuse. (Schwartz and Sharpe, 2006, p. 4)

Practical wisdom enables adult team members to use judgement and sensitivity, as well as expertise and skill. In other words, they can demonstrate qualities not articulated in job descriptions such as kindness, compassion or humanity. This may mean ignoring rules or directives when other people's needs are involved, or improvising in new ways to deliver a personalized service. As Schwartz explains, practical wisdom is not born but made, and therefore it is within everyone's reach and applicable to any job: without it, expertise and brilliance mean nothing:

> We have argued that practical wisdom requires the right goals, the right motives, and the relevant experience. It also requires enough flexibility and autonomy so that one can actually do what the situation calls for. Given these requirements, and given the centrality of practical wisdom, as the executive decision maker, to character, it is distressing that modern social trends are conspiring to make wisdom ever more difficult to cultivate. These trends can be organised around two core features: increasing market pressure and increasing bureaucratisation. The pressure to make a profit threatens both skill and will. (Schwartz and Sharpe, 2006, p. 14)

In this sense role models are those members of the adult team who are moral exemplars. They do far more than only apply expertise: they have learned to apply it with flexibility and creativity in the service of others. These members of the adult team have learned to combine their passion with practice to inspire others to want to learn – the love of teaching.

The role of wise guides

Positive change can be achieved as a direct result of members of the adult team finding and sharing knowledge to inform practice and language within schools. Practical wisdom can be developed across the adult team by each member assuming the role of *wise guide*: a self-named representative dedicated to understanding and defending the rights of specific groups. Wise guides may also develop particular strategies to promote specific changes. Primarily, their role is to nurture both skill and will in others, adding humanity and passion to the development and implementation of ideas for successful change.

This role in shared responsibility is critical, because no adult team member should have to rely purely on policy or goodwill for practice to become fairer. Neither should any individual have to address the issues that make them feel uneasy or at risk of alienation. If people are labelled (for example according to age, race or religion), change comes at the price of stereotyping. Equally it is important to address wellbeing from a number of perspectives, as pitting different causes against each other creates a 'most deserving' mentality that can polarize action and might further marginalize members of the adult team. Put simply, racism should ideally be addressed by white members monitoring the language or practice that might put undue pressure on their black colleagues. In the same way, disablism might be addressed with the help of an adult team member from a different organization if there are no disabled people in the school. Once the information is understood, the non-disabled guides will seek to facilitate the recruitment of a disabled member of the adult team.

This process successfully broadens the team's expertise. Listening to the different voices in the adult team is not always comfortable, but it is essential if change is to benefit each individual member. The strength to hear others' stories is vital. In particular, the process challenges those in positions of power who feel that their own status is threatened by feedback on what they have done. Emotions can run high, so trust and honesty must be nurtured. Deliberately creating self-represented roles is a good way of sharing power and makes trust more explicit within the team. Where different individuals are trusted to take the lead in different ways, teams can share accountability for their learning.

Discrimination is often passive and can only be resolved by action on the part of all team members. All too often, people act on impulse to contradict, ridicule or deny the reality of unfairness and the feelings it creates. The strength of *guides* lies in their detachment from the personal issues without losing the emotional energy to see progress. For them, the real prize is the culture that arises from mutually beneficial learning:

One place where researchers have found strong benefits of happiness on the job is in the area of organizational citizenship. Organizational citizenship behaviours are the tasks workers engage in that help the business and co-workers, but which are not formal duties of their job. These include lending a hand to co-workers, promoting the organisation, and noticing where improvements can be made. (Diener and Biswas-Diener, 2008, p. 75)

Seen in this way, the role of *wise guides* is to develop organizational citizenship by giving each team member the authority to put ideas into practice. The school viewed in this way becomes a more effective *learning organization*, with different members working as guides on different issues. Acting as peer-mentors and taking turns in different areas, adults share with others the skills and behaviours that enable them to flourish. Working together further strengthens the synergy and adds a feel-good factor too, helping all to thrive. Passion is important: when guides speak out they provoke a sense of urgency, the emotion in their voice could be the catalyst that takes others from seeing to feeling, giving them the desire to go the extra mile. Without feeling there is no imperative for action, no sense of purpose for tackling systematic discrimination. In addition, positive energy has an impact on the negativity of those who prefer to ignore these issues and who should be held accountable for holding others back. Negativity exists here at others' expense, by imposing outdated ideas or refusing to move towards better practice that fosters wellbeing.

While outside agencies can provide information and a framework for addressing the issues, a school solution is always more effective. By developing the understanding themselves, guides are more able to provide a perspective that is both locally relevant and personally inspiring. After all, it would be hard to find anyone untouched by at least one of the following: poverty, lack of social mobility, gender discrimination, childhood deprivation, difficult economic position, sexual discrimination, threatened life expectancy due to health inequality, employment shortages or restricted education opportunities.

Fuel for change – creativity and adult play

All work and no play! Adults need play as much as children do. It is a lifelong activity that brings many personal and social benefits. On a personal level play provides a medium for physical and emotional release, positive feelings and creativity. Socially, play in groups offers opportunities to share, practise new skills and experiment with different ideas. Play gives energizing pleasure and develops the mutual trust so important to collaboration. According to Brown (2005), the opposite to play is depression. Brown explains that babies learn about joy through play with their mothers. The sole purpose needed is enjoyment in the activity and a sense of wellbeing. Playing with objects, on the other hand, is vital for developing dexterity and those who lack this experience will find problem solving and physical tasks more difficult.

Play must not be confused with organized games or making work activities fun. Play is spontaneous and intrinsically worthwhile. When play is not contrived or used as a means to an end, the rewards are high. An absence of play can lead to serious problems, from lack of physical and social skills to mental health issues. In children, lack of play can lead to insecurity and aggression. In adults, short tempers and intolerance are likely. Such insight may have implications for the team's wellbeing and the prevention of difficult situations.

When adults play they interact differently, trust, and empathy and cooperation develop, paving the way for successful working relationships. Adults relate more honestly and openly when shared activity is playful. The behaviour and language of play tends to be friendly, less hierarchical and more familial. While workplace language and behaviour often communicate rank and status, play levels the field and decreases the power differential between people. This break from organizational hierarchy allows people to feel safer together, a factor critical to a sense of belonging. Often a hard feeling to explain, belonging is a powerful contributor to team experience. Playing together is enjoyable and pleasure adds to mutual appreciation and deeper acceptance, and thus increasing tolerance. By moving from shared activity to shared feelings, others are acknowledged and respected, but play needs to be *experienced* for belonging to happen.

The shared activity of play allows a joint direction to emerge instinctively. As they work together, people often experience a natural drive to move in step with each other. This natural attraction to others is created by the awareness of a neighbouring individual. As the bond deepens and empathy spreads, the relationship becomes more meaningful even though it may necessarily represent friendship. From the adult team perspective, this allegiance or fondness can lead to trust and provides a solid community foundation. Even in difficult circumstances, play is non-threatening and can enable people to find and make connections. From a social point of view, play brings people closer, and laughing or joking together often helps in stressful situations.

For the adult team, play will be important in the development of new ideas which require creativity and vision. Play also has an essential role in curiosity. Robinson (2009) describes how watching plates spinning was a key moment in Richard Feynman's life that led to his groundbreaking work in quantum physics:

I kept continuing to play with it in a relaxed fashion I had originally done and it was just like taking the cork out of the bottle – everything just poured out, in very short order I worked the thing out for which I later won the Nobel Prize. (Robinson, 2009, p. 70)

In terms of being able to create different ways of working, play has, as we previously identified, a role regarding relationship with reality theory. Sharing dreams and positive scenarios is important for everyone. Play allows people to dream these different scenarios and fantasise beyond their normal barriers. The shared aspect of the process means that new ideas are more likely to arise. Playfulness can effectively innovate and create success. By allowing structured time for enjoyable, shared activity – time that is separate from teaching and planning duties – may help to reignite the passion of all adult team members in the school. Enthusiasm feeds a thriving school and inspires the love of learning.

Diener and Biswas-Diener (2008) refer to the love of learning as a *calling* which energises people to take part in after-work activity. When the barriers between work and leisure are less marked, adult team members are more likely to enjoy activities otherwise perceived as beyond the call of duty. This is important since community involvement often includes activities across personal and organizational boundaries.

Solitary play is as important to personal creativity and imagination as social play, and should not be confused with other passive activities. Opportunities to reflect, dream and imagine are important as they allow individuals to entertain new possibilities that may be instrumental in positive change.

Meaningful relationships

It is relatively easy to share dreams and visions with colleagues who are friends and have similar ideas. However, working with those who have very different visions demands different skills, including confidence in one's own ideas and an ability to accept the perspectives of others. We have discussed how relationships in the adult team are the lifeblood of the school, by turning dreams into experience and giving real meaning to organizational communications and culture. Multi-agency teams pose greater challenges, but the benefits they bring are considerable:

We need also to ensure it has strong, effective and supportive leadership and management at all levels within the system, and that it is able to work comfortably in inter-agency and multi-disciplinary teams. (DCSF, 2007b, p. 152)

Such overarching relationships deepen a school's connection to its community and locality. Without the personal relationships that link people from different organizations, the community ties are fragile and the school may be perceived as working in hostile isolation. The level of engagement within other agencies will determine the level of community influence, and the level of influence will be directly proportional to the quality of the relationships and interactions within the adult team. We gauge the value of an organization according to the welcome, acceptance and honesty of the individuals within it. The modelling and facilitation of relationships must therefore be a primary responsibility of the whole adult team.

Enjoy and achieve

Where schooling seeks only to deliver the knowledge needed to pass tests, achievement is inevitably jeopardized. This narrow approach to 'academic progress' pressurises the adult team, and may stifle creativity, passion and learning. Viewed in this way, learning and progress have only limited value. The systematic limitation of options and choice offers far less than a more holistic route to adult progress and wellbeing. A flexible and creative approach to the teaching role, far broader than simply increasing analytical, linguistic and mathematical ability, also provides possibilities for development and lifelong learning.

This approach is fundamental to the overall goal. Few people are lucky enough to be in jobs that suit their *calling* so perfectly that their work allows them fully to flourish. As Robinson (2009) explains, for those with a *job orientation*, work may simply fill the purpose of funding their outside-work activities. Even so, there is no reason why the passion and enthusiasm created by these interests could not be put to better use. As we identified earlier, a wider range of opportunities to apply knowledge and skills can be hugely beneficial to all learners. Using interests as learning experience would serve a double purpose for adults. First, it enthuses, increasing the pleasure and engagement so important to happiness and wellbeing. Second, many activities allow hands-on application of theory learned in more conventional lessons and may add new elements of creativity and innovation with passion. Indeed, more rounded learning experiences could be pivotal in developing and retaining committed members of the adult team. They also offer children a more realistic view of working life in which passion and skill come together to deliver effective services and products – and even beauty and pleasure. More importantly, by developing their interests within the school, the adult team members are enabled to add elements to their work that are more aligned to their *calling*.

Who is happy?

We have seen that subjective wellbeing scores are closely linked to people's feelings of happiness. If schools can determine wellbeing levels for children by asking them how happy they are, it would make sense to ask also the adult team how happy they are. By asking adults which changes have improved the pleasure, engagement and satisfaction they derive from their work, schools will be in a better position to assess which changes are successful.

A menu for thriving

The pressures of consumerism affect adults as well as children and their health is increasingly threatened by the negative effects of individualistic social habits. Factors that endanger the adult team's health are linked to modern-day living and the responsibility of providing for others. Individualism blurs the boundaries between needs and wants, and adds to the feelings of inadequacy felt when comparing oneself to media icons and celebrities. Seeing the increase of material wealth as a right (regardless of the needs of others) can skew people's priorities. Others' wellbeing becomes the collateral damage of individual success.

The same ideas apply to life balance in schools as to the adult team. Poor diet, long working hours and physical underactivity cause considerable stress and reduced health for most. The factors that help the adult team to flourish are further diminished by the performance culture, e.g. burdensome paperwork causes stress and isolation. Opportunities for varied, mutually beneficial activity are sometimes rare, particularly when the role of teacher has traditionally been seen as solitary activity – one teacher, one classroom. It is important that efforts are made to increase shared activity and the many benefits it brings:

Studies have long shown that taking part in a group activity can improve confidence, self esteem and the ability to relate to other people in a social setting. It can also break down isolation – both a cause and a result of depression – and give people purpose. (Jackson, 2009, p. 5)

Physical and emotional wealth

If physical and emotional wealth is the personal strength enabling individuals to flourish, such wealth in the adult team is best understood as **the joint capacity that enables a group to thrive**. It means that each member of the adult team bears some responsibility for making sure that the whole group gets what it needs. Ultimately, every member should be able to engage freely in every aspect of shared learning – physical, emotional and spiritual. A thriving environment both allows individual members to work together and do well, and to contribute to the group's flourishing.

In order to flourish, all the adult team members need to understand personal wellbeing and apply the same ideas to shared practice. If all members of the adult team understand what they need to flourish and can contribute to the wellbeing of others, then the resulting change in practice can help the whole school to become a thriving entity. In the successful school, the personal development of each member of the adult team contributes towards achieving shared goals, and an adult team which cooperates in this way becomes a positive role model for the pupils. It also enables every adult to take a more active role in the wider community by representing the school. As the team strengthens, it is better able to reach out and consolidate its links with the community. This is a virtuous cycle. As relationships deepen, people feel increasingly valued, safe and wanted. A shared approach sees all community members growing in strength and confidence together. The feeling of belonging increases and the value of the whole community adds up to far more than the sum of individual skills and qualities. Both individual and community wellbeing are enriched.

Balance and extremes

The demands of targets and results on every teacher and practitioner should not be allowed to cost their physical and mental health. Balance is fundamental to healthy lifestyles for adults as well as children. Physically and emotionally resilient adults are capable and positive, allowing them to more fully engage in school life and stand strong in the face of pressures created by the system.

Diversity and range

As we have seen, the strength of the shell – the school – depends on the strength of relationships at both group and individual levels. Teachers and practitioners need, therefore, to work collaboratively with children in the school and other adults outside it. Visions may differ but shared purpose is essential and the adult team should find time and space to develop the language, knowledge and skills that support the shared goal of wellbeing:

> Building on this quality and capacity, we need to ensure that the children's workforce unites around a common purpose, language and identity, while keeping the strong and distinctive professional ethos of different practitioners in the workforce ... Integrated working is pivotal to a personalised service that responds to individuals' needs in a seamless and timely manner. (DCSF, 2007b, p. 152)

Collaboration is not always supported by school organization. The adult team must find ways to share information, techniques and activities, and widen understanding across the whole school. In Chapters 7 and 8 we discussed how children need to lead more in teaching through peer-mentoring and mixed ability activities. Here we explore how the adult team can work in new ways. If the overarching aim is to enable the wellbeing of every child within the school, then the first step is to recognize that the wellbeing of all adults must be addressed. Members of the adult team are also equal learners and their relationships will affect the success of the learning organization. Ultimately, new working practices will help define alternative indicators which, unlike targets defined by exam results, avoid the academic hierarchies that cause so much pressure.

Optimum and maximum

Pursuing 100 per cent along one continuum becomes increasingly less productive; engaging in different activities is often more worthwhile. Moving from an intermediate to a proficient level is just as rewarding as rising from proficient to gifted, although the effort required becomes greater the higher the bar is raised. Therefore, adding to school activities in two ways will not only deliver on target but will also provide greater satisfaction for the adult involved. Furthermore, if the second activity is not a core subject, but is one that stirs passion and enthusiasm, everyone wins (Robinson, 2009).

Team integrity

The strength of the adult team is ultimately dependent on the degree of collaboration between members, their ability to specialize and their capacity to value each other's contribution in realizing joint goals. The adult team should be comprised of people with very different skills, who are able to treat each others' knowledge generously and respectfully. It is gratifying when a vision is shared but, as Lumby and Coleman (2007) observe, this does risk marginalizing the contributions of other ideas and groups. To overlook the needs of any member may prove the downfall of the community.

Ownership and contribution together achieve the conditions in which groups thrive. Although there are few schools under teacher and practitioner ownership, the following principles may be applied to the management of the adult team:

> At the most fundamental level, Gallup management really believes in its workers, so much so that the company is employee-owned, the cafeteria is subsidised . . . there is no official sick-time policy; workers are expected to take time off as needed. The result is a staff of committed individuals who enjoy their work, make friends at the office and stay loyal to the company. (Diener and Biswas-Diener, 2008, p. 76)

However, creating an environment of responsibility requires greater attention to adults' ability to thrive. As we have seen, a 'wealth model' based on balance and integrity can nurture high aspiration. It contrasts with a standards culture in which deficits are 'plugged' in order to reach a specified performance level.

Thriving teams

Deliberate cultural change requires more than understanding. Each member of the adult team needs to deliberately seek the transformation needed to secure wellbeing for the whole school. Organizational structures and systems must change in order to better support greater wellbeing. At the same time, tackling inequality in small ways also impacts on culture: the *right* changes make work easier for everyone:

> The respect that is inherent in some high status jobs, however, can be extended to all jobs, even lower status ones, in the best organisations. When customers, co-workers, and management treat you well, it is likely that you feel your work is worthwhile. Good workplaces are those that have opportunities for respect and status built into all jobs. (Diener and Biswas-Diener, 2008, p. 79)

To achieve equality of status, it is essential to think clearly about the bigger picture – that is, the ideology that has become so detrimental to success. Small changes will only be effective if they actually address the wider issues. They must not be seen as change for change's sake, but a key step in an enduring and broader transformation that will benefit society. A society that is struggling due to excess demands a more complex approach to the problem than an increasing celebration of high performance.

11 Implications for leadership

This final chapter explores the various ways in which the discussion so far impacts on our understanding of how effective leadership works. In particular, this chapter develops a model of school leadership that is both sensitive and responsive to the various issues raised in previous chapters. Three themes will dominate this discussion: the implications for our understanding of moral leadership of a social justice perspective; the concept of social entrepreneurship as the basis for leadership strategies; and the contribution of the concept of social pedagogy to redefining the role of leadership.

Moral leadership

Educational leadership might be thought of as ethics in action. It is difficult to conceptualize a situation where leadership could be seen as morally neutral, indeed it is probably not an exaggeration to claim that there is no situation where an educational leadership decision does not have direct and explicit moral implications. As we hope has been demonstrated throughout our discussion, issues around equity and equality permeate every dimension of educational life from the design of school buildings to policies on inclusion to the nature of teaching and learning strategies. Leadership is so important in this context because of the disproportionate impact that leaders have on the way in which educational organizations work. It is both a great strength and a weakness that one person can have such an influence on the values, culture and operation of such a complex organization as a school.

Frequent reference has been made in earlier chapters to the Scandinavian countries and their approach to social and educational matters. It therefore seems appropriate to start this discussion by examining the publicly stated commitment to values of the Finnish teacher's trade union, i.e. this is not an imposed government agency's view.

Human worth
A humanistic conception of people and a respect for human beings form the underlying basis of ethical principles. The worth of a human being must be respected regardless, for example, of the person's gender, age, religion, origins, opinions or skills.

Honesty
Honesty to oneself and in all one's interactions forms the foundations of the teacher's work.

Justice
In relations between the teacher and group or the individual learner, as well as in the activities of the rest of the work community, justice must prevail. Justice encompasses equality, the avoidance of discrimination and favouritism, the opportunity to be heard and the right to resolve conflicts.

Freedom
The point of departure for all social relations, however, is respect for the freedom that is intrinsic to a human being's worth.

Teacher and pupil
The teacher accepts the learner and strives to consider him or her as a unique individual.

Teacher's relationship to work
In their work, teachers commit themselves to the norms that define that work, and to the profession's ethics. Teachers attend to their tasks responsibly. Teachers develop their work and evaluate their own activities. Teachers accept their fallibility and are ready to revise their viewpoints. (OAJ, nd, pp. 3-4)

This substantial extract from *The Teacher's Professional Ethics* (nd), published by Opetusalan Ammattijarjesto (OAJ) the Trade Union of Education in Finland, provides a powerful example of how a political, cultural and social commitment to social justice is reflected in a rich set of professional/moral propositions which point to a clear hegemony within society. What is also clear is the importance of a shared language which helps to clarify the underpinning concepts that inform professional action.

It would be impossible to demonstrate an exact correlation between these principles, Finland's performance relative to other education systems and the levels of social wellbeing and effectiveness found in Finland. However, it does seem remarkably auspicious that the only teacher's union produces an ethical code which reads as a manifesto for social justice in a liberal democracy. There is obviously a tension between articulating and defining explicitly the types of expectations in the Finnish code and what might be seen as taken for granted and assumed principles. However, without explicit articulation it is difficult to see how any degree of alignment, consensus or consistency might be achieved.

There is a very clear agreement in the research and in the literature of educational leadership that morally motivated leadership is one of the most powerful forces in securing high performance schools and a wide range of valued education outcomes. This raises important 'how?' and 'what?' issues. What are the characteristics of morally driven leaders and what particular permutation of values should they pursue? In the context of this book, the authors are convinced that leadership for social justice is the only valid way forward. The relationship between values and leadership is confirmed by a National College for School Leadership research project which explored the variables that explain outstanding headship. The most significant factor to emerge to explain outstanding headship was a strong personal faith, philosophy or vocation:

> For many of the respondents, educational leadership is, at its most fundamental level, a moral activity. 'Everybody has worth ... I do believe that every child has worth and we have to create an environment to bring that out.' (West-Burnham, 2009, p. 5)

Without this type of commitment it is difficult to see how education in general and schools in particular can begin to address the sorts of issues discussed in this book. Leadership for social justice requires a balance of very clear and well formulated beliefs about the nature of equality and equity, and the ability to translate those beliefs into the concrete experience of those most directly affected. Leadership for social justice is very much about modelling appropriate behaviours and developing a common vocabulary to enable meaningful dialogue across the community:

> Modern societies will depend increasingly on being creative, adaptable, inventive, well-informed and flexible communities able to respond generously to each other and to needs wherever they arise ... And, because we are trying to grow the new society within the old, our values and the way we work must be part of how we bring a new society into being. (Wilkinson and Pickett, 2009 p. 263)

Social entrepreneurship

Social justice requires action. Moral indignation or aspirational platitudes do not provide appropriate responses to the issues that a lack of social justice generate. What the authors have sought to develop throughout this book are examples of how very real and practical is the lack of social justice, and so the remedy has to be proportionately real and practical. We have provided a range of practical examples of how we feel various aspects of social injustice might be addressed. However, many aspects of social injustice move beyond the personal and organizational and it is at this stage that it is necessary to move into social and community action:

> Social entrepreneurs worth their salt do not follow conventional ways of working. Their view of the world begins with people, passion, experience and story – not policy, statistics and theory. (Mawson, 2008, p. 2)
>
> Social entrepreneurs know from hard-won experience that the trick is first to demonstrate what you are proposing to do for people in a small and tangible way and then expand the sense of possibility. (ibid. p. 3)
>
> What marks out social entrepreneurs from business entrepreneurs and other kinds of charitable and public sector workers is that they are not driven solely by financial profit or ideology, or by a career or a pension scheme ... They feel that they have something important to share that must be demonstrated both emotionally and practically. (ibid. p. 7)

Figure 11.1 attempts to expand and analyse Mawson's view of social entrepreneurship by contrasting it with other types of social and economic activity. The classification and descriptions of the different domains will obviously be a caricature, but there are certain broad categories which might help to explain the different working cultures, structures and processes in the various areas of activity.

Perhaps the most compelling and distinctive feature of social entrepreneurship is that it is responsive to real local need rather than imposing generic solutions or assuming that agencies know better than their clients. It is the focus on solution-based strategies and relevant projects that gives social entrepreneurship its potential impact and ability to build capacity and sustainability. Social entrepreneurship might be best understood as combining or reconciling personal and organizational motivations that are normally seen as mutually exclusive (e.g. profitability and a moral perspective), for example being driven by values but seeking to remedy social injustice in a 'business-like' way. As can be seen in the model in Figure 11.1, social entrepreneurship reconciles a range of imperatives, principles and strategies from other types of human enterprise. The key characteristics of social entrepreneurship can be summarized as follows:

- There is a clear moral purpose, usually based around social justice/ inclusion issues but the solutions are expressed in commercial terms.
- Funding is derived from multiple sources for the same project.

Commercial entrepreneurship	Social entrepreneurship
Market driven	Values driven, commercial reality
Customer focus	Mixed funding – project focus
Economic pricing	Mixed staffing/community engagement
Organizational ethos	Innovative approach to social need
Consumer/shareholder orientation	Calculated risk
Managed risk	Social value
Economic value	Collaboration not competition
High competition	

Charitable work	Government agencies
Moral/transformative purpose	Policy driven/short term outcomes/disjointed incrementalism
Funded through giving	Treasury funded
Volunteers working altruistically	Professional silos
Engaging with marginal groups	Low risk
Low corporate risk/high personal risk	Public value
Moral value	Limited competition
No competition	

Figure 11.1 Understanding social entrepreneurship

- Staffing is highly varied and pragmatic, i.e. full-time employees, part-time workers, volunteers.

- The culture is one of openness; inclusion, creativity and innovation – good ideas are accepted on face value not ideologically constrained.

- Projects are very carefully managed to minimise the risk of failure and maximize the possibilities of success.

- The criterion for success is the extent to which the project/activity adds social value, i.e. improves and enhances the quality of people's lives.

- One of the key distinguishing features of social entrepreneurship is that it is open and inclusive, and not driven by ideological or competitive requirements.

One of the issues for school leaders working for social justice is that much of their organizational life has been spent working in the context of a governmental culture. There may be advantages in school leaders engaging with charities (beyond the ritual humiliation that is often required in the name of fundraising) and securing business expertise (e.g. project management or customer focus) – but *not* becoming business people. Collins (2006) makes the reasons for this very clear:

> We must reject the idea – well intentioned, but dead wrong – that the primary path to greatness in the social sectors is to become 'more like a business.' Most businesses – like almost anything else in life – fall somewhere between mediocre and good. Few are great. When you compare great companies with good ones, many widely practiced business norms turn out to correlate with mediocrity, not greatness. (p. 1)

For Collins, the issue is not one of the transferability of concepts across sectors but rather the overarching commitment to his vision of greatness: 'We need to reject the naive imposition of the language of business and instead jointly embrace a language of greatness' (ibid. p. 2). This is why the moral perspective is so important in social entrepreneurship; in this context greatness is defined as social justice, equity and inclusion.

Social entrepreneurship reconciles what are often seen as competing imperatives and does so in a way that captures the best of each: the moral passion of charity work; or the ability to deliver of the commercial sector with the accountability of the public sector. An example of how this might work is the Fifteen Foundation – the restaurants founded by the chef Jamie Oliver to provide opportunities for disadvantaged young people. The restaurants work to the highest professional standards and are in business to make a profit but they also have the potential to change people's lives and life chances. Successful business entrepreneurs are usually people who either develop a new product or service or reinvent an existing way of operating. Entrepreneurship is often synonymous with innovation. Social entrepreneurship therefore needs to focus on social innovation rather than product innovation: According to Geoff Mulgan (cited in Walker, 2009) attention is now turning:

> ... to investing systematically in social creativity, whether in relation to climate change, ageing or the challenges of hyperdiverse cities. Few dispute the need to invest in technological innovation. But more are now recognising the need for much broader strategies, for 'recovery through innovation'. (p. 1)

We are very used to innovation in technology and in many ways we have come to expect and celebrate it. Innovation in terms of social and community issues is much more challenging. Reconfiguring the role of the school and its relationship with the wider community will often require a fundamental reappraisal of long-held beliefs. Social innovation involves questioning the often unspoken hegemony of social beliefs and stereotypes, roles and relationships, and the structures and processes that govern our day-to-day assumptions and activities. Collins (2006) stresses the importance of leaders of social ventures making a deliberate choice to be in control and exercise leadership through proven strategies for success. Rather than seeking social justice through political, legislative and judicial approaches, it may be more appropriate to seek to change actual practices, to change employment practices, to model genuine inclusion in schools, and to demonstrate equity in community provision:

> If social change lies in the alignment of shifting practices, structures and beliefs, then these approaches are promising because they can simultaneously tackle all three. There is nothing as effective in revealing and unsettling deep-rooted cultural prejudices as encountering an experience which quite clearly refutes the basis on which they have been held. (Young, 2006, p. 67)

Social pedagogy

Social pedagogy is concerned with the learner in context. The classic view of pedagogy is that of the theory and practice of teaching and learning, which is almost totally driven by the interplay between that which is to be taught, who is to teach it and to whom it is directed. In its crudest form, pedagogy takes no account of the various and complex variables that actually determine the success or failure of a particular lesson. Social pedagogy, by contrast, recognizes that the learner is not in a vacuum: social issues are highly significant in determining the success of any educational process whether an individual lesson or a phase of schooling. Social pedagogy is therefore about the learner in context and the learner as person. This relates to the idea that education cannot be a 'socially neutral' process; it is impossible to discount the social and personal variables that every learner brings to every learning situation and context. Social pedagogy might be best understood through the following elements:

- A holistic focus on the person, recognizing and respecting the dignity and significance of that person in personal, social and cultural terms.
- An active engagement with the person seeking to understand and develop an effective relationship with them on their terms.
- Recognition of the need, as appropriate, for restorative and compensatory intervention to build personal capacity.
- Embedding the relationship in a framework of rights, entitlement and the value and dignity of the individual.

In many European countries social pedagogues are a quite distinct professional group who may be thought of, in crude terms, as combining the work and values of teachers and social workers. Their work is concerned with children who need support in overcoming social disadvantage or problems by developing a sense of personal efficacy, self-identity and esteem, and the capacity to act independently.

Social pedagogues reconcile and integrate the academic with the relational, the intellectual with the emotional and the personal with the social. In some ways social pedagogues could be seen as a possible future expression of the movement in England towards the full expression of *Every Child Matters*. If social justice is to be even a remote reality then those involved in the education of young people and children may have to come to perceive themselves as primarily social pedagogues with leadership changing accordingly. In their discussion of leadership and social entrepreneurship Leadbeater and Mongon (2006) provide guidelines which reconcile the three main themes of this chapter, leadership needs to be:

> ... self-effacing and stressing the contribution of others – leading through persuasion and consensus ... (recognizing) that that the public sector alone cannot solve social problems. The recognition that complex social problems need partnerships and alliances to solve them has implications for the congruent style of leadership. Alliances and networks need leaders who are politically astute, good at listening and drawing out the contributions of others, and provide an overall sense of direction without dominating. (p. 242)

Leadership for social justice is very hard work; not least because there are many in contemporary British society who would deny the relevance of need for such an approach. Because of its complex and multi-faceted nature, social justice in education can easily be compromised, diluted and diminished. It is very easy to argue for multiple alternative perceptions – social justice is contingent on time and place and is always concerned with minorities. It takes courage to oppose this reductionist view and assert that social justice is an absolute – it cannot be compromised because it is about the very essence of our humanity.

Afterword

So that's the theory! What about the people? This afterword is written from the perspective of a disabled woman: Laura Chapman.

I personally feel that there is point at which too much theory can remove us from reality. The nature of academic dialogues can isolate people, and such divisions of mind can damage the relationship with those worse affected. While injustice within our education system is allowed to continue, a great number of us are paying too high a price for ignorance, inactivity and resistance to change.

Reasoned arguments can desensitize us to the problem. Careful and logical analysis may legitimize the situation when it proves the problem is too big to tackle. Seeking refuge in the privileged position of an unfair system ultimately shields us from engaging with hurt inflicted on others and thereby our own humanity. It helps remove any human connection to those made increasingly vulnerable, the final proof that our greed and egotism has won. While we refuse any part of any action towards greater social justice, we also deny the right for those closest to us to be happy – our children, our partners, our friends and our colleagues. Not wanting to face those we can ignore may take away a sense of responsibility and personal guilt; unfortunately, it is the ultimate insult to those we come into contact with. Dressing up ignorance, and shrouding it in ideology, only serves to dismiss a simple reality – when those we meet are no longer our equals, their lives become less important than ours.

I am keenly aware of the incredible opportunity I was given when asked to co-author this book. This invitation illustrates clearly how social justice can be achieved when people take action to make a difference. An act of wisdom, courage and humanity need not change the world, but in these pages it could change a life. It is rare that a voice such as mine is positively sought, and most often it is ignored, ridiculed or silenced. This rejection, entirely passive, happens when people do not think to act: I am simply not invited to join in. The human cost is that I feel my presence is at best tolerated, not entirely desired and my contribution unwanted. At times I have fought hard to stay involved, at other times I have chosen to leave in order to avoid the pain this causes. Any sense of belonging, therefore, is always precarious and threatened by other people's willingness to recognize my value. In a public way, being one of the authors was a very tangible expression of my professional contribution and ultimately my personal worth.

It is rare that I feel fully valued. I feel my worth is routinely put in question by other people's use of a 'special' label to describe the outsider nature of my voice. Being marked out as a 'disability equality trainer' narrows my professional contribution to very specific ideas: seen as additional or removed from common practice. A lack of academic status and a down to earth approach make me all the more easy to dismiss. Dialogues on social justice rarely invite the 'hard to hear'; high prices and academic snobbery are great barriers to the relationships that would offer change. Furthermore, my appearance ensures that those swayed by image and status instinctively reject what I have to say. This very personal dismissal invalidates the hard work and often the bitter experience I have to share. However unintended, being pushed aside repeatedly is very painful, but more importantly it trivializes any positive contribution I am able to make to the broader context and the more universal aspects of educational change. The final offence is the lack of fair pay that fuels this negative cycle many feel they will never escape.

It all started at school, and remembering those days is still a very unpleasant experience. Not wishing to undervalue the friendships that made it bearable, the overriding memory is still a raw and painful one. It is not that school, college and university were austere or harsh – we had **all** mod-cons: our own duvets, plenty of choice at meal times, and no-one was beaten! However, life for some of us was characterized by a deeper and subtler humiliation, a pernicious prejudice, often apparent in the forms of bullying that were tolerated: elitism, academicism and ableism. While despondency for those on the receiving end was often the norm, the overall experience was a far cry from the 'pleasant life' we all had a right to. I remember feeling that school was a time to be endured, and worse than this I was often told that the future would not be much more attractive. Motivation was often extinguished by the pessimism that could be seen in teacher's eyes, a mix of pity, blame and resignation in the face of the bleak situation that faced us all. Wider injustice was rationalized in order to be made acceptable, as it was easier to point out the personal deficiency than work towards a remedy to the injury. The message was clear: 'You'll always have to work harder than others – so you better get used to it.' This hands-on-ears approach to the issue of my participation provided an easy out for those in a position to help. Some teachers could choose to justify their apathy: 'social justice – not my problem'. Looking back, periods of illness provided respite from the stress of having to compete on unfair grounds. From an adult perspective, I wonder how the unhappiness could have been ignored? I would not be so hurt if things had significantly changed but, speaking with young people today, they face the same attitudes. They are equally demotivated by adult pessimism, and this lack of belief in their abilities denies the very aspiration they have a right to.

In light of this, I wanted to make it abundantly clear that this book was not written as an act of revenge for the hurt inflicted or the abuse endured. There were those whose intent I question to this day, but they were very few. The teachers I got to know were good people – friendly and caring – and I have no doubt their intention was to make life good. However, the integration of a disabled child, back then, went so far beyond the accepted norm as to be outside the role of teacher or the even the purpose of education. Schools were designed to get you jobs, and disabled people did not get jobs, therefore I did not need educating. The changing reality was deeply troubling and rocked people's ideas of teaching far too radically.

This book has only been possible thanks to those that accepted the challenge. Despite difficult circumstances, many did take on the job of adapting to wider social change. Furthermore, they did it with enthusiasm: they broke the rules, bucked the system and redefined convention. The wisdom they demonstrated went way beyond the role, the duties and the job description. These were teachers whose passion provided all children with the hope and optimism so vital on the journey to success. It is with these *wise guides* in mind that I set about writing, without much understanding at the time for the sheer scale of the work involved, but with a high degree of confidence that was to prove invaluable.

It might sound harsh to say that these were not special people, as they will always be very special to me. They were ordinary people changing the world one life at a time. They chose to make a difference by ensuring ordinary practice was typically extraordinary. If only every teacher had felt able to do this, how different things might have been! Thank you Mlle Baret, Roget, George, Jack, Barrie ...

References

Ainscow, M. and Dyson, A. (2006) *Improving Schools, Developing Inclusion (Improving Learning)*, London: Routledge

Alexander, R.J. (2009) *Towards a New Primary Curriculum: A Report from the Cambridge Primary Review. Part 2: The Future*, Cambridge: University of Cambridge Faculty of Education

Archard, D. (2004) *Children: Rights and Childhood*, Abingdon: Routledge

Ashcroft, J. and Carroe, P. (2005) *Thriving Lives: Which Way for Wellbeing?* Relationships Foundation, online at: www.relationshipsfoundation.org/download.php?id = 171

Batty, D. (2008) UK slips further down global gender equality league, *Guardian*, 13 November, p. 13

BBC Online News (2009) Warning over youth mental health, 5 January, available at: http://news.bbc.co.uk/1/hi/health/7810902.stm

Beck, I and Stanovich, K. (2000) *Progress in Understanding Reading: Scientific Foundations and New Frontiers*, New York: Guildord Press

Berthoud, R. (2006) *The Employment Rates of Disabled People*, Leeds: HMSO

Block, P. (2008) *Community: The Structure of Belonging*, San Francisco, Calif.: Berrett-Koehler

Booth, R. (2008) Gap between rich and poor narrows ... , *Guardian*, 22 October, p. 6

Brooks, L. (2006) *The Story of Childhood: Growing Up in Modern Britain*, London: Bloomsbury Press

Brown, S. (2005) Speech on TED talks, available at: www.ted.com/

Bruce, T. (2001) *Learning Through Play: Babies, Toddlers and the Foundation Years*, Abingdon: Hodder & Stoughton

Bunch, G. (2005) *10 Keys to Successful Inclusion*, Dehli: North South Dialogue, online at: www.marshaforest.com/tenkeys.pdf

Burchardt, T. (2005) Just happiness? In Pearce, N. and Paxton, W. (eds) *Social Justice: Building a Fairer Britain*, London: Politico's Publishing

Children in Scotland (2006) Child poverty review, available at: http://child-policyinfo.childreninscotland.org.uk/index/news-app?story = 2896

Children's Society (2009a) *Good Childhood? A Question for our Times*, London: Children's Society

Children's Society (2009b) *What Gives Children and Young People a Good Childhood?*, London: Children's Society

Collins, J. (2006) *Good to Great and the Social Sectors*, London: Business Books

Csíkszentmihályi, M. (1996) *Creativity*, London: Harper Perennial

Curtis, P. (2008) Half of pupils below poverty line get no free school meal, *Guardian*, 16 December, p. 12

Dalai Lama and Cutler, H.C. (1998) *The Art of Happiness: A Handbook for Living*, London: Coronet

DCSF (2007a) Report of findings from the DCSF 'Time to Talk' Consultation Activities, London: Department for Children, Schools and Families (www.dcsf.gov.uk)

DCSF (2007b) *The Children's Plan*, London: Department for Children, Schools and Families

DCSF (2007c) *Safe to Learn: Embedding Anti-bullying Work in Schools*, Nottingham: DCSF

Department for Children, Schools and Families (2008) *Guidance for Schools on Promoting Pupil Wellbeing*, Department for Children Schools and Families, available at: www.dcsf.gov.uk/consultations/index.cfm?action = conResults&consultationI-d = 1564&external = no&menu = 3

DfES (2005) *Excellence and Enjoyment: Social and Emotional Aspects of Learning Guidance*, London: DfES Publications (www.standards.dfes.gov.uk)

Diamond, J. (1998) *Guns, Germs and Steel*, London: Vintage

Diener, E. and Biswas-Diener, R. (2008) *Happiness, Unlocking the Mysteries of Psychological Wealth*, London: Blackwell Publishing

Dixon, M. and Paxton, W. (2005) The state of the nation. In Pearce, N. and Paxton W. (eds) *Social Justice: Building a Fairer Britain*, London: Politico's Publishing

Dweck, C. (2006) *Mindset The New Psychology of Success*, London: Random House

Early Childhood Forum (2003) PowerPoint presentation.

Evans, G. (2006) *Educational Failure and Working Class White Children in Britain*, Basingstoke: Palgrave Macmillan

Filer, J. (2008) *Active and Outside, Running an Outdoors Programme in the Early Years*, Abingdon: Routledge

Fullan, M. (2007) *The NEW Meaning of Education Change*, New York: Columbia University

Gardner, H. (1993) *Multiple Intelligences\; The Theory in Practice*, New York: Basic Books

Geddes, H. (2006) *Attachment in the Classroom, the Links between Children's Early Experience, Emotional Wellbeing and Performance in School*, London: Worth Publishing

Gilbert, D. (2005) TED talks 2005, available at: www.ted.com/

Gilbert, D. (2006) *Stumbling on Happiness*, London: Harper Perennial

Gladwell, M. (2008) *Outliers the Story of Success*, London: Penguin Books

Goldenfield, N., Baron-Cohen, S., Wheelwright, S. (2005) Empathising and systemising in males, females, and autism, *Journal of Neuropsychiatry*, 2(6), 338–45

Grimston, J. (2009) Cure for the Facebook generation, 1 February, online at: http://women.timesonline.co.uk/tol/life_and_style/women/families/article5627605.ece

Hargreaves, A. and Fink, D. (2005) *Sustainable Leadership*, San Francisco, Calif.: Jossey-Bass

Harvey Wood, H. (2008) *The Battle of Hastings*, London: Atlantic Books

Hawken, P. (2007) *Blessed Unrest: How the Largest Movement in the World Came into Being, and Why No One Saw It Coming*, New York: Viking

Healthy Schools (2009) The Healthy Schools Programme, online at: www.healthyschools.gov.uk

Helgesen, S. (1995) *The Female Advantage, Woman's Ways of Leadership*, New York: Doubleday

Hills, J. Sefton, T. and Stewart, K. (2009) *Towards a More Equal Society*, Bristol: The Policy Press

Hirsch, D. and Spencer, N. (2007) *Unhealthy Lives End Child Poverty*, online at: www.poverty.org.uk

HM Treasury (2003) *Every Child Matters: Green Paper*, London: The Stationery Office

Huppert, F. Baylis, N. and Keverne, B. (2005) *The Science of Well-being*, Oxford: Oxford University Press

Isaacs, W. (1999) *Dialogue and the Art of Thinking Together*, New York: Doubleday

Jackson, L. (2009) In active pursuit of mental wellbeing, *Guardian*, 18 February, p. 5

James, O. (1998) *I Britain on the Couch*, London: Arrow Books

James, O. (2007) *Affluenza*, Reading: Vermillion

Kline, N. (1999) *Time to Think: Listening to Ignite the Human Mind*, Oxford: Ward Lock, Cassell Illustrated

Layard, R. (2005) *Happiness: Lessons from a New Science*, London: Penguin Books

Layard, R. and Dunn, J. (2009) *A Good Childhood, Searching for Values in a Competitive Age*, London: Penguin Books

Leadbeater, C. and Mongon, D. (2006) *Leadership for Public Value*, Nottingham: NCSL

Lumby, J. with Coleman, M. (2007) *Leadership and Diversity: Challenging Theory and Practice in Education (Education Leadership for Social Change)*, London: Sage Publications

Magadi, M. and Middleton, S. (2007) *Severe Child Poverty in the UK*, London: Save the Children's Fund (www.savethechildren.org.uk)

Margo, J. and Dixon, M. (2006) *Freedom's Orphans: Raising Youth in a Changing World*, London: IPPR

Mason, M. and Dearden, J. (2004) *Snapshots of Possibility: Shining Examples of Inclusive Education*, London: Alliance for Inclusive Education

Mental Health Foundation (2009) *Mental Health, Resilience and Inequalities*, London: Mental Health Foundation

Mawson, A. (2008) *The Social Entrepreneur*, London: Atlantic Books

Mittler, P. (2004) *Working Towards Inclusive Education: Social Contexts*, London: David Fulton Publishers

Mundy (2007) Private conversation

National College for School Leadership (2009) *Personalising Learning*, online at: www.ncsl.org.uk/personalisinglearning

National Institute for Play (2006) http://nifplay.org/index.html

Nettle, D. (2005) *Happiness, the Science Behind your Smile*, Oxford: Oxford University Press

NHS/DCSF (2008) *PSHE Education Guidance for Schools*, November

Noguera, P. (2008) *The Trouble with Black Boys*, San Francisco, Calif.: Jossey Bass

Nussbaum, M. (2006) *Frontiers of Justice*, Cambridge, Mass.: Belnap Harvard

OAJ (nd) *The Teacher's Professional Ethics*, Finland: Opetusalan Ammattijarjesto (OAJ)

Office of the United Nations High Commissioner for Human Rights (OHCHR) (2009) Convention on the Rights of the Child, online at: www.11million.org.uk/

Ofsted (2006) *School Inspection: A Guide to the Law*, online at: www.ofsted.gov.uk/Ofsted-home/Forms-and-guidance/Browse-all-by/Other/General/School-inspection-guide-to-the-law-part-1

Palmer, G., MacInnes, T. and Kenway, P. (2007) *Monitoring Poverty and Social Exclusion*, York: Joseph Rowntree Foundation

Pollock, L. (2009) Fit for purpose, *Guardian*, 18 February, p. 4

Pont, B., Nusche, D. and Hopkins, D. (2008) I*mproving School Leadership: Volume 2 Case Studies on System* Leadership, Paris: OECD

Putnam, R.D. (2000) *Bowling Alone*, New York: Simon & Schuster

Rawls, J. (1971) A *Theory of Justice*, Cambridge, Mass.: Harvard University Press

Robinson, K. (2001) *Out of Our Minds: Learning to be Creative*, Mankato, Minn.: Capstone

Robinson, K. and Aronica, L. (2009) *The Element: How Finding Your Passion Changes Everything*, London: Allen Lane

Robinson, K., McDermott, S. and Scase, R. (2005) *The 3 Gurus: Live in London* (Audio CD), Red Audio Professional

Russell, J. (2008) We've forgotten to teach social skills, and our children are stagnating, *Guardian*, 8 November, p. 5

Schwartz, B. and Sharpe, K. (2006) Practical wisdom: Aristotle meets positive psychology, *Journal of Happiness Studies*, 377–95

Seligman, M. (1995) *The Optimistic Child, A Proven Programme to Safeguard Children Against Depression and Build Lifelong Resilience*, New York: Houghton Mifflin Company

Seligman, M. (2002) *Authentic Happiness, Using the New Positive Psychology to Realize your Potential for Lasting Fulfilment*, London: Nicholas Brealey Publishing

Seligman, M. (2005) Speech on TED talks 2005, available from: www.ted.com/

Shah, H. and Marks, N. (2004) *A Well-being Manifesto for a Flourishing Society*, London: New Economics Foundation

Shepherd, J. (2009) Universities don't like common people do they?, *Education Guardian*, 3 March, pp. 1–2

Tashie C. (nd) PowerPoint presentation

Taylor, M. (2006) It's official: class matters, *Education Guardian*, 28 February, p. 1

Toynbee, P. (2008) Signs of progress at last, but profound inequality remains, *Guardian*, 4 November, p. 31

Toynbee, P. and Walker, D. (2008) *Unjust Rewards*, London: Granta Books

UNICEF (2007) *Child Poverty in Perspective: An Overview of Child Well-being in Rich Countries*, Innocenti Report Card 7, Florence: UNICEF Innocenti Research Centre

United Nations (2009) Human Rights, www.un.org/en/rights/

Vernon, M. (2008) *Wellbeing* Stocksfield: Acumen Publishing

Walker, D. (2009) Recovery through innovation, *Society Guardian*, 18 March, p. 5

West-Burnham, J. (2009) *Developing Outstanding Leaders* Nottingham, NCSL

West-Burnham, J. & Coates, M. (2005) *Personalizing Learning: Transforming Education for Every Child*, London: Network Educational Press

Wilkinson, R. (2005) *The Impact of Inequality: How to Make Sick Societies Healthier*, New York: The New Press

Wilkinson, R. and Pickett, K. (2009) *The Spirit Level: Why Equal Societies Almost Always do Better*, London: Allen Lane

World Health Organization (2008) *Closing the Gap in a Generation*, Geneva: WHO

Young, R. (2006) For What it is Worth: Social Capital and the Future of Social Entrepreneurship' in Nicholls, A. (ed.) *Social Entrepreneurship: New Models of Sustainable Social Change*, Oxford: Oxford University Press.

Index

salience of boundaries and balance in
creating wellbeing among 98–100
strategies to counteract discrimination
against 51–4
see also children; cultures, learning;
participation, learner; pedagogy
learning, community
strengths in promoting cohesion and
collaboration 119–20
lifespan
influence of social injustice and
inequality 10

meaning (concept)
salience of community participation in
securing 121–2
methods, teaching
impact on educational success of
learners 47–51, 54–8
strategies to counteract learner
discrimination 51–4
see also teams, teacher
mobility, social
influence on social injustice and inequality
7–8
models and theories
'broaden-and-build' 91–2
wellbeing 31–6

nutrition
inequality of and implications for health of
children 64–9

options, curriculum
salience an impact on learner happiness
94–6
organisation, educational
impact on educational success of
learners 47–51, 54–8

participation, community
characteristics, strengths and
weaknesses 114–19
salience in enhancing social inclusion
124–6
strength of liberating culture within 122–4
see also outcomes eg meaning; relationships
see also qualities and types eg collaboration;
learning, community

participation, learner
salience of individual uniqueness 18–19
salience of influence of social equality and
justice 105–9
pedagogy, social
contribution to definition of leadership
role 151–3
play
impact on health and wellbeing of
children 80–6
need and importance within teacher teams
136–8
poverty
impact on educational success of
vulnerable children 40–42
impact on understanding of health and
wellbeing 59–60
influence on social injustice and
inequality 7, 9
prejudice
impact on educational success of
vulnerable children 42–4
prevention within teaching teams 129–31
see also discrimination
prevention, disease
balance as element in ensuring 63–7
salience of strategies in creating healthy
society 60–61
projects, community
characteristics and strengths 114–18
strength of liberating culture within 122–4
see also outcomes eg meaning; relationships
'psychology of success' (Dweck) 107
pupils *see* learners
purpose, common
salience within successful teacher
teams 132–4

'relationship with reality' theory 72
relationships
salience of community participation in
enhancing 124–6
salience within teacher teams 138–9
resilience
salience and impact on happiness of
learning 96–7
rights, human
need to secure within teacher teams
129–31